Teaching Archaeology in the Twenty-First Century

Edited by Susan J. Bender and George S. Smith

SOCIETY FOR AMERICAN ARCHAEOLOGY

This publication was supported by a grant from the Getty Grant Program.

The Society for American Archaeology, Washington, D.C. 20002
Copyright ©2000 by the Society for American Archaeology
All rights reserved. Published 2000

Printed in the United States of America

Cover design by Victoria Russell, Paper Tiger Studio.

Photo credit: cover —C. Vance Haynes presents a geoarchaeology workshop to the
1997 University of Wyoming field school students, crew, and volunteers at the Hell Gap site
(courtesy Mary Lou Larson, the University of Wyoming)

Teaching Archaeology in the Twenty-First Century/edited by
Susan J. Bender and George S. Smith

Library of Congress Catalog Card Number: 99-64920
ISBN No. 0-932839-15-0

TABLE OF CONTENTS

acknowledgments

Without the support and contributions of numerous organizations and individuals this project and the resulting report would not have been possible. We would like to thank the SAA's Public Education Committee within which many of the ideas that gave life to this effort were born. By establishing the Task Force on Curriculum, the officers and Board members of SAA provided valuable direction and support for this project. Organizational sponsorship and support was provided by the Archaeological Institute of America, Bureau of Reclamation, American Anthropological Association, Canadian Archaeological Association, National Park Service (Southeast Archeological Center and Archeology and Ethnography Program), National Association of State Archaeologists, Society for American Archaeology, and Society for Historical Archaeology. In addition, these organizations also provided representatives who participated in the Wakulla Springs Workshop and/or served on the Task Force on Curriculum. Their participation made possible a diverse approach to the issues at hand.

Many individuals have contributed to this effort. We would like to thank those who responded to the departmental and student surveys and those who provided comments and suggestions via the electronic Bulletin Board. These contributions were critical because they provide perspectives on the issues from a wide and diverse audience, including archaeologists from governmental, private, and academic settings as well as from students preparing for careers in archaeology.

The individuals involved directly in the workshop and task force were a joy to work with. They participated by preparing position papers and providing in-depth and well- conceived comments on various issues directly related to this report. Their willingness to serve and contribute accounts for much of the success of this project. Specifically we would like to acknowledge the hard work and contributions of the following individuals: Jeffrey H. Altschul, David G. Anderson, Judith R. Bense, Dennis Blanton, Tobi A. Brimsek, Noel Broadbent, Elizabeth Brumfiel, Kathleen Byrd, Elizabeth Chilton, Pamela Cressey, Hester A. Davis, Nancy DeGrummond, Glen Doran, John Ehrenhard, Ricardo Elia, Maria Franklin, Dorothy Schlotthauer Krass, Shereen Lerner, Mark J. Lynott, Bob McGimsey, Chip McGimsey, Frank McManamon, Phyllis Mauch Messenger, Regina Meyer, Jim Miller, David Pendergast, David Pokotylo, K. Anne Pyburn, Joseph Schuldenrein, Dean Snow, Vincus P. Steponaitis, Joe Watkins, and Nancy White. Without their knowledge, dedication, and friendship, this report would not have been possible. We would like to acknowledge the support and understanding of the Getty Grant Program for funding the production and distribution of this report.

Susan J. Bender and George S. Smith

● ●

foreword

Dean R. Snow

At the end of the twentieth century, we American archaeologists find ourselves with the happy problem of managing our success. When I first started reading about archaeology a half century ago, it was an esoteric pursuit followed by a few struggling professionals and a supporting cast of avocationals. Since then the numbers of professional archaeologists in colleges, universities, and museums have mushroomed. But importantly the number of nonacademic professional archaeologists has grown even more, to the point that more than half of us now work in nonacademic positions. Before complaining to others about having to adjust to these new circumstances we should consider how much sympathy the wealthy receive for the tribulations of managing their money. Such is the price of success.

A small but representative number of archaeologists met in Wakulla Springs, Florida, early in 1998 to explore strategies for success management. At least some of us came prepared for vigorous and protracted dispute. This, I suspect, was conditioned by years of experience as minority members of anthropology departments. Many of us were astonished to discover instead that there was broad consensus even before serious debate got started. The conference moved quickly to the business of making recommendations after finding little to argue about in the earlier stages.

It boils down to this. Academic archaeologists have long designed their programs to produce more academic archaeologists, a default strategy still followed by many other disciplines as well. Many of us in academic departments with doctoral programs still aspire to raise the next generation of professors and place them in the best academic positions. Meanwhile, the market for professional archaeologists is increasingly a nonacademic one, and the key credential for entry into the majority of open positions is the M.A. or M.S., not necessarily the Ph.D. A glance at the salary range for MBAs should provide sufficient evidence for the efficacy of professional programs at the master's level.

Not every student wants or needs a doctorate to become a professional archaeologist. Many currently leave doctoral programs early, using their master's degrees to enter the profession. At Wakulla Springs we tried to craft recommendations that would restore value and utility to B.A., M.A., and M.S. degrees, and that would make them more than just stepping stones to the Ph.D. Many of us may still aspire to educate the next generation of the professoriate, but we recognize that some of them will follow other paths. But even if those of our students who do replace us in academic posts do not require new program structures, surely their students will.

Archaeology is a much grander profession than it was a half century ago. It has many more parts than it once had, and it is time for us to begin managing our wealth before we are embarrassed by it. The Wakulla Springs Conference has given us a start. I am convinced that if we follow the conference recommendations we will promote a profession built on an array of quality programs at the bachelor's, master's, and doctoral levels. I can think of no finer legacy to pass on to twenty-first century archaeology.

I.

Background
History of the Issues

HISTOᖇICAL BACKGᖇOUND: THINKING ABOUT HOW WE TEACH AᖇCHAEOLOGY

Susan J. Bender

This section explores the structure and content of graduate and undergraduate archaeolgoy curricula in the late twentieth century. A theme uniting the following papers is that traditions of academic training have not kept pace with changing contexts for the practice of archaeology. Indeed, several authors imply that traditional conceptualizations of archaeology as an academic or liberal arts discipline has acted as a countervailing force against acknowledging and incorporating the wider contexts of archaeological practice into courses focused on conveying the method, theory and subject matter of the discipline. McGimsey and Davis argue, for example, that all archaeological practice is public, yet our curricula traditionally pay scant attention either to training future professionals to work in the public arena or to developing an awareness of how this arena shapes the production of archaeological knowledge.

Krass points out, furthermore, that such lapses can be traced to the fact that our curricula have not changed significantly in structure since the mid-twentieth century when the discipline quite explicitly characterized itself as a scientific research profession. The pedagogies associated with teaching a discipline so conceptualized traditionally emphasize coverage of up-to-date content, building from lecture- to seminar-style learning. Within this framework, students are expected to "know their stuff" and learn to conduct research by modeling their professors' accomplishments. Issues of how students might apply their research knowledge outside of an academic context and the broader ethical considerations surrounding the conduct of research are usually considered peripheral to the central curricular principle: teaching the content and method of the research discipline. For the undergraduate context in particular, the traditions of liberal arts education—emphasizing the rigors of intellectual training with little explicit reference to broader applications of knowledge and skills developed within the disciplines—have been a mainstay of such a curricular structure.

However, as William Lipe points out, archaeology can no longer be taught as if it were solely a research discipline. While the research function of the discipline—generating new knowledge about the past—remains its central feature, the contexts for doing so are increasingly funded and scrutinized by the public. We must train future professionals to operate successfully in this context, even as we work toward educating a public that is both supportive and appropriately critical of such research. It is time to critically assess the history of teaching archaeology and ask ourselves the contemporary question of what knowledge, skills, and abilities our students should possess once they leave the academy and go on to function as professionals and educated citizens within our communities. This is surely the path that leads toward ensuring the well-being of our discipline into the twenty-first century.

THE OLD ORDER CHANGETH

or,
Now that Archaeology is in the Deep End of the Pool, Let's Not Just Tread Water

Charles R. McGimsey III and Hester A. Davis

Since the publication of *Public Archaeology* (McGimsey 1972) more than 25 years ago, truly massive changes in the face and practice of archaeology have taken place.

In the first 25 years after World War II, the number of individuals employed in archaeology grew markedly while the number of nonteaching positions probably hovered around 100. Today, Zeder reports that the number of archaeologists in nonteaching positions accounts for over one-half of the profession, a percentage that suggests numbers well into the thousands (1997:46).

This dramatic alteration in the relative importance of employment sectors within the profession has not resulted in the development of some "new" element or aspect of archaeology, something that we might call Public Archaeology. Rather, over these last 25 years, archaeologists have come increasingly to recognize, utilize, and serve their various publics more effectively—publics which were there all along (cf McManamon 1991). As McGimsey has said, "There is no such thing as 'private archaeology'" (1972:5).

Public archaeology, as we see it, entails the effective coordination, encouragement, and integration of all who wish to participate in, contribute to, and benefit from all aspects of archaeological work. Only insofar as archaeology becomes effective public archaeology can the creation and maintenance of appropriate public attitudes occur, which in turn permits decisionmakers (or cultural resource managers, among others) to develop and apply the legal and administrative mechanisms and the funding necessary for participants in archaeology of all persuasions to work effectively together to achieve archaeology's three basic goals: 1) maximum conservation of the archaeological resource base, 2) derivation of the maximum amount of information from that base, and 3) communication of the results of that conservation and research to the largest possible public audience.

In short, it is our contention that public archaeology is not some kind of "add on." It IS archaeology. Without this approach to practicing archaeology, there can be no future for archaeology.

On the other hand, cultural resource management is an aspect of archaeology that *has* developed for the first time in the last 25 years (except for those few archaeologists who worked in the Park Service prior to 1972). It is not that "management" has not always been a proper part of archaeology; it is simply that before the development of an adequate database and historical preservation law, archaeological management in any meaningful sense, was impossible.

It should be obvious to all of us that doing archaeology today and in the foreseeable future is vastly different from doing archaeology prior to 1974. And we assume that it is equally evident that what students are being taught today has not kept pace with the changes. Spurred by the changes enacted with the 1974 Archaeological and Historical Preservation Act, two books were published in 1977. Both King et al., and Schiffer and Gummerman, commented briefly about "training," essentially recommending that graduate students needed to have "additional" courses in law, planning, devising a research design for a client, and preparing budgets. At the 1974 CRM conference in Denver, Jesse Jennings said maybe a "crash course" of 6 to 8 weeks should be developed to provide archaeologists with information not covered in their graduate program. Indeed, a few universities instituted what were essentially CRM tracks for their M.A. program, and several of them remain to date. Many graduate programs started teaching at least *one* course called "public archaeology" or "cultural resource management," and as evidenced by the survey results reported by Smith and Krass in this volume, a few still maintain these courses in their curricula.

In 1986, Davis (reported in 1989) performed a superficial survey of anthropology departments and found that several of those who had instituted CRM tracks in the mid-1970s had abandoned them 10 years later. No one was taking the courses (compare with Blanton, this volume); during that period, the job market blossomed and freshly minted M.A. archaeologists were able to get a job without the "extra" courses! Business practices, competition, "downsizing" in federal projects, and other factors have resulted in leveling off the huge increase in jobs of the 1974-1984 decade. At the same time, of course, Lipe's (1974) "conservation ethic" and the more public orientation in the practice of archaeology became the accepted way to "do" archaeology. But "doing" archaeology today is not just science, or just management, or just technique. It is all these things at once and the curriculum provided for prospective students (both undergraduate and graduate programs) must take these points into account.

The survey reported in this volume (Smith and Krass) tells us that although faculty who construct academic programs are aware of these demands, they have by and large not reworked their curricula accordingly. Academic programs, particularly at the doctoral level, are still oriented to providing students with the same kind of content and research skills provided to professors who trained 25 years ago—theory, method, and area courses; a course or two in sociocultural anthropology; and perhaps even linguistics or bioanthropology. McGimsey (1994) has suggested that one way to adjust to the needs of the new challenges to archaeology might be to develop courses such as "cultural anthropology for archaeologists." Perhaps some "core courses" serve this purpose, but not those we know about. It is time for some truly innovative thinking about how to provide the essential information that will properly equip potential archaeologists in the twenty-first century—*not* the mid-twentieth century.

We repeat that academic programs should not be modified simply by grafting a handful of new requirements onto the present curriculum. Rather, we recommend a complete reworking of all anthropology programs from the starting point of defining the basic information needed by undergraduate majors and the emergent professionals in our graduate programs. In this exercise, we need to focus on creating integrated curricula that provide in *each* individual course (be it "method and theory in archaeology," or "Indians of North America") information on understanding archaeological ethics and law, delivering information for and to various publics, interacting with Native Americans, and applying anthropological principles and theory to real-world situations. Only in this approach to their curricula will anthropology departments produce professionals better prepared to find an appropriate and satisfying career in whatever arena that can use their talents.

Moreover, it is essential to note that the approach to rethinking curricula that we advocate here is rooted in our long-held conviction that public archaeology is the archaeology of the twenty-first century and that public archaeology is not CRM. Rather, cultural resource management is one niche in which archaeologists, historians, historic preservationists, and anthropologists can apply the information they acquire from the renovated curriculum we envision.

In reviewing the changes in professional practice over 25 years and the initiatives that spurred them, we have been struck by the fact that those which were successful were not those ending in a report read by a few (e.g., regional research centers, Marquardt 1977; standards for CRM, Bense et al. 1986), but rather those that led to widely read publications whose recommendations were enacted (e.g., *The Airlie House Report*, McGimsey and Davis 1977; *Stewards of the Past*, McGimsey et al. 1969; *Archaeology and Archaeological Resources*, McGimsey 1973). The purpose of this volume is to bring the initiative to change the teaching of archaeology to the broadest audience possible and to encourage dialogue about such change and a desire to act. The purpose of this paper has been to set forth some central themes to guide such change.

References Cited

Bense, J.A., L. Heartfield, K. Deegan, and H. A. Davis
   1986   Standards and Guidelines for Quality Control in Archaeological Resource
   Management in the Southeastern United States. *Southeastern Archaeology*
   5(1):52-61.

Davis, H. A.
   1989   Learning by Doing: This is No Way to Treat Archaeological Resources. In
   Archaeological Heritage Management in the Modern World, edited by H. F.
   Cleere, chapter 27. Unwin Hyman, London.

King, T. F., P. P. Hickman, and G. Berg
   1977   *Anthropology in Historic Preservation: Caring for Culture's Clutter.*
   Academic Press, New York.

Lipe, W. D, and A. J. Lindsay Jr. (editors)
   1974   *Proceedings of the 1974 Cultural Resource Management Conference.* Technical Series 14. Museum of Northern Arizona, Flagstaff.

McGimsey, C. R. III
   1972   *Public Archaeology.* Academic Press, New York.

   1973   *Archaeology and Archaeological Resources: A Guide for Those Planning to
   Use, Affect, or Alter the Land's Surface.* Society for American Archaeology,
   Washington, D.C.

   1994   Yin and Yang and Archeology's Future. *Society of Professional Archaeologists Newsletter* 18 (10): 1-4.

McGimsey, C. R. III, C. H. Chapman, and H. A. Davis
   1969   *Stewards of the Past.* Arkansas Archaeological Society and Missouri
   Department of Agriculture, Fayetteville, Arkansas.

McGimsey, C. R. III, and H. A. Davis (editors)
   1977   *The Management of Archaeological Resources: The Airlie House Report.*
   Special Publication. Society for American Archaeology, Washington, D.C.

McManamon, F.P.
   1991   The Many Publics for Archaeology. *American Antiquity* 56:121-130.

Marquardt, W. H.
   1977   *Regional Centers in Archaeology: Prospects and Problems.* Research Series
   14. Missouri Archaeological Society, Columbia.

Schiffer, M. B. and G. J. Gummerman (editors)
   1977   *Conservation Archaeology: A Guide for Cultural Resource Management
   Studies.* Academic Press, New York.

WHAT *IS* THE ARCHAEOLOGY CURRICULUM?

Dorothy Schlotthauer Krass

W hen we talk about an archaeology curriculum that needs to be renewed, we are invoking the traditionally shared North American approach that views archaeology as the study of the human past through the material record; that developed as a discipline in museums, research universities, and liberal arts colleges through the twentieth century; and whose students were assumed to be either incipient archaeologists who also would work in museums or academia, or individuals whose lives in other professions or careers would be enriched by a systematic examination of past human experience and accomplishments. What does that traditional curriculum look like, and why does it take the form it does?

Two collections of writings particularly illustrate the thoughtful construction of this curriculum, its goals, and its varied format. It is, of course, not a uniform or proscribed set of courses or readings. Archaeologists are proud of their independence—in fact, one of the goals of the discipline has been to foster independent thinking and the breaking of new ground (in more than one sense of the metaphor). But this variability in academic approaches can be—and has been—described in larger terms, and it is useful to look again at how the curriculum has been imagined by the outstanding archaeologists who contributed to a mid-century discussion of *The Teaching of Anthropology* (Mandelbaum et al. 1963a), and to a recent volume, *The Teaching of Anthropology: Problems, Issues, and Decisions* (Kottak et al. 1997), devoted to "examining, updating, reevaluating, and enlarging the issues discussed in" the 1963 collection (Kottak 1997:1).

The Curriculum in 1963

The six archaeologists who wrote chapters in the section on "The Teaching of Anthropological Archaeology" in the 1963 volume—David Baerreis, Robert Braidwood, Jesse Jennings, Alfred Kidder, Gutorm Gjessing, and Richard Woodbury—share the assumption that the archaeology curriculum was a liberal arts curriculum. Woodbury talks about the contributions that archaeologists have made "to the general body of knowledge that should be part of every person's intellectual acquisitions at the college level, if not earlier" (Woodbury 1963:229). Jennings describes the "special function of teaching archaeology" as "giving the student, through archaeological materials, an intimacy with the past and

with the whole world of man and culture" (Jennings 1963:251).
The authors also share a common picture of the structure of the curriculum—a picture most of us would recognize as the archetype against which we measure what we are doing. Gjessing (in a chapter that focuses on the dangers of nationalism and chauvinism) provides a short description of the ideal structure:

> ...teaching can best be organized in three stages: 1) introductory courses of general anthropology, including ecology and some elementary principles of scientific method, with a certain emphasis on the archaeological and, hence, on the culture historical aspect; 2) general principles and methods of archaeology, focusing on one or two larger areas; 3) specialization in a more or less restricted field, according to the student's particular interests [Gjessing 1963:266].

Kidder, in his chapter on "Course Design" and Braidwood in his on "Themes and Course Progression" write in greater detail, describing the content and the goals of courses at each level. An introductory-level course serves as a enriching experience helping students (regardless of major) to understand the breadth, depth, diversity and complexity of human history. It also may serve as an appetizer, encouraging some students to sample more archaeology courses and recruiting some into the major and the profession. Jennings, in his chapter on "Educational Functions," describes this course as the opportunity to take the student's "curiosity about antiquity for its own sake" and "transmute it into systematic inquiry...to impart some depth and breadth and systematic understanding of man's behavior" (Jennings 1963:247).

Kidder's curriculum would follow the introductory course with a method-heavy course focused broadly on one or another large part of the world (e.g., Introduction to Old World Archaeology) and made compelling by the teacher-researcher's expertise and passion for his subject. Braidwood's second step is an "introductory-advanced course" addressing "great problems" (from the emergence of tool-making, culture-bearing beings, to the appearance of urbanized, politically formalized societies, with attention to the mechanics of cultural transmission and change, and the changing relations of man, society, environment, and culture).

Both Kidder and Braidwood then assume that the greater part of an archaeologist's education will take place in "area courses" of increasingly narrow focus and increasingly sophisticated analysis. They see area courses as including both archaeology and ethnography, not as specialized archaeology courses. They do not see a role for upper-division courses on archaeological method and theory. Theory is anthropological theory, and methods are best taught in the field. As Baerreis puts it in his article on teaching techniques, "The professional archaeologist learns his discipline through field and laboratory experience, since there is no substitute for what amounts to apprenticeship under a skilled practitioner" (Baerreis 1963:253).

In this context, Baerreis also cautions that working as a laborer on a river basin survey is no substitute for a structured field school (Baerreis 1963:258). This is one of the rare references in the 1963 articles to the work that archaeologists do after, or outside of, the classroom. The other reference to the conduct of archaeology outside of the academy is Braidwood's statement that working at a private university meant he was under no pressure to engage in "salvage archaeology" (Braidwood 1963:244). Elsewhere, the emphasis is on archaeologists as researchers "...because this is the basis of their reputations and professional advancement" (Woodbury 1963:233) and as professionals who represent archaeology to their students and the wider public.

The Context for the Curriculum

Some perspective is required here about the size and shape of the archaeological community in which the 1963 authors were working. The Society for American Archaeology (SAA) was then a constituent organization of the American Anthropological Association, the publishers of the 1963 volume. SAA had approximately 2,000 members in 1963, 360 of whom attended the Annual Meeting at Boulder, Colorado. Members voted to raise the annual dues from $8 to $10 for 1964, and set the registration fee for the 1964 meeting at $2 (Society for American Archaeology 1963: 270-278).

The program for the 1963 meeting included 21 symposia, with 135 individuals presenting papers or acting as chairs. University and college affiliations predominated: 87 (64 percent) of the participants representing 44 institutions. Next came museums and research centers with 32 individuals (24 percent) representing 19 institutions. Third came governmental agencies (state and federal—excluding museums) with 12 individuals (9 percent) representing 5 institutions. Finally: 4 independent individuals (3 percent) presented papers as well.

When the second curriculum volume was published the late 1990s, SAA had approximately 6,000 members, and annual meetings regularly attracted about half that number—quite a contrast to the 18 percent who attended in 1963. The institutional affiliations of members had also changed considerably. A survey of SAA members in 1987 and a larger census of archaeologists in 1994 show a larger proportion of archaeologists in the government and private sectors and a decrease in the proportion in museums and academia (Zeder 1997:45-47). In 1994, 42 percent of the respondents to the SAA census indicated their primary workplace was academic, for 10 percent it was a museum, for 27 percent it was a government agency, and for 21 percent it was in the private sector.

The Curriculum in 1997

Given this change in the shape of the archaeological workplace, how has it affected the archaeology curriculum?

The archaeologists writing in the 1997 volume on teaching anthropology (James Deetz, George Michaels and Brian Fagan, Stephen Plog and Fred Plog, and Patricia Rice) share the 1963 assumption that the teaching of archaeology is to enrich the undergraduate liberal arts curriculum and perhaps to recruit majors. Several authors note that the students come from a more educationally and socially diverse background, and that they have had a wider array of educational experiences in their K-12 schooling. But not one of the archaeologists addresses the changes in career trajectories for archaeologists that will send more of these majors into contract and management archaeology than into research and teaching. (not even Fagan, who has been eloquent on the topic elsewhere—e.g., his 1999 article in *Discovering Archaeology*).

This change is not unnoticed elsewhere in the same volume. In his introduction, Conrad Kottak explicitly points out the *"People, especially men, who earned Ph.D.s in anthropology in 1963 expected to have graduate students and research support."* And *"Many, perhaps most, Ph.D. anthropologists will never train a graduate student"* (Kottak 1997:3, emphasis in the original). Kottak goes on to describe the changes in teaching conditions—from research institutions to institutions "where teaching schedules are heavy...and where research is not only unsupported but discouraged" (Kottak 1997:3). Neither he nor the anthropologists who write in the "Applied" section nor the archaeologists mention the large numbers of archaeologists who will not be in teaching positions of any kind.

In fairness, articles in the 1997 volume each focus on one exemplary course, and none sets out to describe the archaeology curriculum in the way Braidwood and Kidder did in 1963. The Plogs' discussion of the "Central Themes in Archaeology" focuses on the large picture of what archaeology can contribute to the understanding of human history and social behavior. Their "central topics" are in the tradition of Braidwood's "great problems" in 1963, and they conclude by setting the teaching of archaeology firmly in the liberal arts tradition:

> If there is a single theme to be addressed in prehistory, it is why in a very few times and places large and highly normative populations developed and why some persisted for only a few hundred years while others lasted for thousands. Only by addressing this basic theme will we confront the fragility of the societies and institutions that we see around us and take to be enduring [Plog and Plog 1963:221].

The chapters by Deetz, Michaels and Fagan, and Price each describe an introductory course. Deetz emphasizes the need for each instructor to organize this course around his or her own experience, expertise and enthusiasm. Except perhaps for his explicit (and appropriate) inclusion of historical archaeology, the course he describes could fit easily into the sequences described in 1963. Price's "Participant Archaeology" describes involving the students in activities that force them to reach conclusions themselves. She emphasizes the pedagogical rewards of starting from the specific (activities) and moving toward the general, and makes a compelling case that innovative teaching does not have to depend on big budgets or big staffs.

Michaels and Fagan, on the other hand, describe using the latest in modern high-tech tools to re-create the introductory course at a large university, with teaching assistants, multimedia consultants, and a computerized campus. Their student-centered course de-emphasizes lectures but increases the contact between instructors and students, and encourages the students to take more responsibility for their own learning. In this narrative, the authors never discuss the content of the course, so it is difficult to know how, or if, their teaching reflects or incorporates the changes in the careers of archaeologists.

The 1997 volume does extend the range of students who are being taught archaeology. It contains a whole section on "Teaching Anthropology to Precollegiate Teachers and Students" which has no parallel in the 1963 volume. Chapters by Dennis W. Cheek, Norah Maloney, and Ruth Selig in this section include the teaching of archaeology. And, as the Price and Michaels and Fagan articles demonstrate, more attention was being paid to the effectiveness of teaching and the appropriateness of pedagogical techniques. But the reader might come away from the 1997 volume with the idea that curriculum *as a whole* has not been subject to the same degree of examination as the pedagogy.

That examination is the topic of the discussions in this volume.

References Cited

Baerreis, D. A.
  1963   Teaching Techniques. In *The Teaching of Anthropology,* edited by D.G. Mandelbaum, G. W. Lasker, and E. M. Albert, pp. 247-252. Memoir 94. American Anthropological Association, Washington, D.C., and University of California Press, Berkeley.

Braidwood, R. J.
  1963   Themes and Course Progression. In *The Teaching of Anthropology,* edited by D.G. Mandelbaum, G. W. Lasker, and E. M. Albert, pp. 239-246. Memoir 94. American Anthropological Association, Washington, D.C., and University of California Press, Berkeley.

Deetz, J.
1997   Introductory Archaeology: An Identity Crisis in the Temple of Doom. In *The Teaching of Anthropology: Problems, Issues, and Decisions*, edited by C. P. Kottak, J. J. White, R. H. Furlow, and P.C. Rice, pp. 232-239. Mayfield, Mountain View, California.

Fagan, B.
1999   An Academic Time Warp: New Archaeologists Don't Fit the Job Market. *Discovering Archaeology* (July/August):8-11.

Jennings, J. D.
1963   Educational Functions. In *The Teaching of Anthropology*, edited by D.G. Mandelbaum, G. W. Lasker, and E. M. Albert, pp. 247-252. Memoir 94. American Anthropological Association, Washington, D.C., and University of California Press, Berkeley.

Kidder, A. II
1963   Course Design. In *The Teaching of Anthropology*, edited by D.G. Mandelbaum, G. W. Lasker, and E. M. Albert, pp. 233-238. Memoir 94. American Anthropological Association, Washington, D.C. and University of California Press, Berkeley.

Kottak, C. P., J. J. White, R. H. Furlow, and P.C. Rice (editors)
1997   *The Teaching of Anthropology: Problems, Issues, and Decisions*. Mayfield, Mountain View, California.

Kottak, C. P.
1997   Introduction: The Transmission of Anthropological Culture Today. In *The Teaching of Anthropology: Problems, Issues, and Decisions*, edited by C.P. Kottak, J. J. White, R. H. Furlow, and P.C. Rice, pp. 1-12. Mayfield, Mountain View, California

Mandelbaum, D. G., G. W. Lasker, and E. M. Albert (editors)
1963a   *The Teaching of Anthropology*. Memoir 94. American Anthropological Association, Washington, D.C., and University of California Press, Berkeley.

Mandelbaum, D. G.
1963b   The Transmission of Anthropological Culture. In *The Teaching of Anthropology*, edited by D.G. Mandelbaum, G. W. Lasker, and E. M. Albert, pp. 1-21. Memoir 94. American Anthropological Association, Washington, D.C., and University of California Press, Berkeley.

Michaels, G. H., and B. M. Fagan
1997   The Past Meets the Future: New Approaches to Teaching Archaeology. In *The Teaching of Anthropology: Problems, Issues, and Decisions*, edited by C. P. Kottak, J. J. White, R. H. Furlow, and P.C. Rice, pp. 239-246. Mayfield, Mountain View, California.

Plog, S., and F. Plog
1964   Central Themes in Archaeology. In *The Teaching of Anthropology: Problems, Issues, and Decisions*, edited by C. P. Kottak, J. J. White, R. H. Furlow, and P.C. Rice, pp. 218-222. Mayfield, Mountain View, California.

Rice, P.
1965   Participant Archaeology. In *The Teaching of Anthropology: Problems, Issues, and Decisions*, edited by C. P. Kottak, J. J. White, R. H. Furlow, and P.C. Rice, pp. 247-254. Mayfield, Mountain View, California.

Society for American Archaeology
1963   Report of the Annual Meeting. *American Antiquity* 29:270-278.

Woodbury, R. B.
1966   Purposes and Concepts. In *The Teaching of Anthropology,* edited by D.G. Mandelbaum, G. W. Lasker, and E. M. Albert, pp. 223-232. Memoir 94. American Anthropological Association, Washington, D.C., and University of California Press, Berkeley.

Zeder, M. A.
1997   *The American Archaeologist: A Profile*. AltaMira Press, Walnut Creek.

Archaeological Education and Renewing American Archaeology

William D. Lipe

In the United States (and in most other parts of the world as well), "doing archaeology" has become an increasingly complex enterprise during the past 35 years, largely as a result of the growth of public archaeology in all its various manifestations. Archaeology's principal contribution to society remains the provision of new information about the past on the basis of systematic study of the material remains of past societies. In recent years, however, archaeologists also have accepted a responsibility (one shared with a variety of other groups) for stewardship of the archaeological record.

Contemporary archaeology is deeply embedded in social, political, and economic contexts that affect how archaeologists go about their business of information-seeking and stewardship. Access to the archaeological record is regulated and restricted by federal and state laws and policies that take into account a variety of public policy goals in addition to archaeological research. The interests of Native Americans and other groups in the symbolic or heritage aspects of the archaeological record are recognized both legally and in archaeologists' own ethical codes. Funding generated by government agency and private-sector compliance with historic preservation and environmental laws has come to dwarf that provided by traditional grants designed to support pure research. The majority of archaeological fieldwork is now done by private sector consulting firms rather than by universities and museums. Management of the *in situ* archaeological record—including activities ranging from site protection to public education to supervising contracts for various field studies—has become a set of well-developed professional specialties. Curation of records and collections—at least those obtained from public lands or with public funding—is finally being taken seriously, with a concomitant shift of time and money into these activities.

In other words, archaeology and archaeologists are much more a part of the "real world" than was true a few decades ago. The growth of public archaeology has created new constraints on the practice of archaeology, but has also resulted in a tremendous expansion of employment in the field and of its public visibility. Along with that growth have come requirements for greater accountability in the conduct of archaeology. The complex system of laws, regulations, interest groups, and organizations that provides the context for "doing archaeology" has been remarkably effective in raising the public value of archaeological resources, but is plagued with contradictions and inefficiencies. It could be made to work much better.

What is the role of archaeological education in all of this? How can we do a better job of training students to work effectively in the complex and demanding context of modern archaeology? Can better training of archaeologists make the system work better?

Some aspects of these questions have been addressed in recent years by the Society for American Archaeology's Task Force on "Renewing Our National Archaeological Program." Early in 1996, the task force held a small conference to address this large problem. The conference report was widely circulated and then discussed at an open forum at the Annual Meeting in New Orleans. The report and a summary of the comments that were received were published in the *SAA Bulletin* (Lipe and Redman 1996). A follow-up meeting was held in the spring of 1997, and the task force report that resulted was presented to the SAA Board of Directors at the Annual Meeting in Nashville (Lipe 1997). These steps were taken to identify certain important issues, and focus discussion and debate on these issues within the archaeological community. The "Renewing" Task Force hoped that its work would be a catalyst for productive change.

One of the five main topics in the 1996 task force report was "Increasing Professional Knowledge and Expertise at all Levels of Archaeological Resource Management." In this section, the task force expressed the opinion that "...many of the problems experienced in the national archaeological program were not failures of system or process, but of judgment exercised by practitioners, whether they be resource managers, regulators, or researchers. It was felt that increasing the professionalism of personnel throughout the system would increase its effectiveness and accountability" (Lipe and Redman 1996). In this section of the report, the task force made two recommendations. One dealt with the need for wide acceptance of professional standards of qualification, performance, and ethics. The other recommendation dealt with training. Here, the task force recommended that "Training should be improved for archaeologists entering the CRM field, whether as consultants, regulators, or resource managers. The knowledge, skills, and abilities (KSA) required for these positions should be assessed, and both academic and on-the-job training should be modified to ensure that these KSA are effectively taught" (Lipe and Redman 1996). A number of thoughtful comments on the topics of training and professionalism were received in response to this section of the report (Lipe and Redman 1996).

The 1997 task force report (Lipe 1997) again took up the issues of training and professionalism. The report recognized that there is a great lack of uniformity across American archaeology in what is accepted as adequate professional training and performance. It urged that the profession of archaeology "establish a standard of professionalism, assist individuals in obtaining the knowledge, skills, and abilities to attain and maintain that standard, and implement a process whereby archaeologists are held accountable to appropriate standards and qualifications" (Lipe 1997). The standards of research performance and code of ethics of the Society of Professional Archaeologists (now the Register of Professional Archaeologists or RPA) were recommended as a base upon which to build a more uniform approach to professionalism. The task force recommended that the SOPA (now RPA) or equivalent professional standards for archaeologists be adopted by agencies and institutions involved in public archaeology, and that the major archaeological and historic preservation organizations encourage their members to qualify for registration under SOPA (now RPA). The task force report also suggested that there be a continuing education requirement for registered professionals. It endorsed the concept of standards and registration for field schools (something currently offered under RPA) and suggested that university departments be encouraged to develop professional certificate programs for specialized areas of archaeology.

As noted, the "Renewing" Task Force hoped that its work would serve to focus debate about the strengths and weaknesses of our national efforts in public archaeology and that it would also stimulate a variety of efforts to find ways to improve those efforts. The "Initiative on Teaching Archaeology in the Twenty-First Century" is exactly the kind of "next step" that we on the "Renewing" Task Force envisioned. We recognized that one of the challenges facing American archaeology today is how properly to train students for the exciting and dynamic—and increasingly complex and demanding—world of public archaeology that most of them will enter if they choose to work as professional archaeologists.

The time that students can realistically devote to formal undergraduate and graduate training in archaeology is limited. Hence, the critical question for college and university teachers is what educational experiences will best equip students to do a good job of archaeological information-seeking and/or stewardship in the complex environments in which they will be working as professionals. It also is obvious that as educators, we cannot simply pack our students full of everything-they-will-need-to-know during the few years they are in school. In addition to giving them specific technical "knowledge, skills, and abilities," we must truly educate them, in the sense of equipping them to continue learning independently and critically, and to be able to modify their work patterns on the basis of what they have learned. Both the technical preparation and the independent learning aspects of education are essential if they are to be productive professionals over a career. The papers in this volume take up these questions with the care, thoroughness, and insights they deserve.

References Cited

Lipe, W.D.

1997   Report of the Second Conference on "Renewing Our National Archaeological Program," February 9-11, 1997. Submitted to the Board of Directors of
the Society for American Archaeology.

Lipe, W. D., and C. Redman

1996   Conference on "Renewing Our National Archaeological Program." *SAA
Bulletin* 14(4):14-17.

SAA Surveys Regarding Public Archaeology/ Cultural Resource Management and Teaching

George S. Smith and Dorothy Schlotthauer Krass

In its continuing effort to obtain information about the current state of teaching cultural resource management/public archaeology, the Society for American Archaeology (SAA) surveyed departments of anthropology as well at students within those departments. The results of these surveys, conducted in 1998, provided background for several discussions for the Wakulla Springs workshop on "Teaching Archaeology in the Twenty-First Century," the national dialogue on curriculum taking place on SAA's Web site, and the ongoing efforts of SAA's Task Force on Curriculum.

Departmental Survey

To understand the current state of teaching about public archaeology and cultural resource management (CRM), SAA conducted a survey of all departments of anthropology in the United States and Canada. The goals were to learn whether public archaeology/cultural resource management is being taught at the collegiate level; whether it is taught in free-standing courses or programs, or embedded in other courses; whether departments have specific plans to add courses or programs; and to identify the perceived obstacles to teaching public archaeology/cultural resource management. Some information about the makeup of departments and the students receiving degrees in archaeology also was solicited. Suggestions also were requested as to ways SAA could help departments include public archaeology/cultural resource management in their offerings.

Hester A. Davis and David Pokotylo developed a questionnaire, which was modified after recommendations by SAA's Committee on Survey Policy. The questionnaire was sent to 343 institutions listed in the American Anthropological Association's *Guide to Departments* (AAA 1997) that included faculty members with specialties in archaeology. Responses in this analysis are from 117 departments, or 34 percent of the departments that received the questionnaire.

Only about one-third of the departments responding offer courses that deal "primarily" with public archaeology/cultural resource management. Forty of the 117 departments offer one or more dedicated courses:

19 of these are undergraduate courses, 19 are graduate courses, and 27 are cross-listed. That only 11 of these courses are taught by adjunct or sessional faculty implies that these offerings are seen as permanent parts of the curriculum, a hopeful indication that there is a base of receptivity for the topic in about one-third of the departments.

It is not surprising that these courses are offered more frequently in the larger, graduate-degree-granting departments than in departments where the highest degree is the bachelor's. Twenty-nine (51 percent) of the 57 graduate-degree-granting departments offer courses primarily about public archaeology/cultural resource management, while only 11 (18 percent) of the 60 undergraduate-only departments do. Self-standing courses, however, are not the only vehicles for teaching public archaeology/cultural resource management. In fact, 98 departments—84 percent of the total response—report they offer courses that include some coverage of these topics at the undergraduate level, and 43 report these issues are included in graduate courses (that is, 76 percent of the departments offering graduate degrees). In addition, 52 departments (45 percent) offer undergraduate internships in public archaeology/cultural resource management, and 23 offer graduate internships (40 percent of the graduate programs).

Another indication that departments are interested in moving their curriculum in this direction is that 71 departments (61 percent of those responding) said there is "sentiment among [their faculty] that it would be useful to develop courses in public archaeology/cultural resource management." Further, 64 (55 percent) said they had specific plans for instituting courses, and 18 (15 percent) said that they had specific plans for instituting a program. This high level of planning may be a biased result, because departments engaged in this kind of planning may have been more inclined to participate in this survey.

On the other hand, when departments were asked to identify the obstacles to teaching public archaeology/cultural resource management courses (see Table 1), the most commonly chosen reason was that "other courses take priority." This was cited by 62 percent of the undergraduate departments and 61 percent of the departments offering graduate degrees. Many undergraduate departments added notes such as, "With a three-person (2 cultural, 1 archaeology) program within a weak social sciences division, we spend much of our effort teaching general education courses." Another said, "We are grossly understaffed with only three to carry an undergraduate major." These comments remind us that this is an important issue that must be kept in mind in any discussion regarding curriculum reform.

In addition, departments with graduate programs cited "lack of faculty interest" as frequently as they cited other priorities. Explanatory comments accompanying "lack of faculty interest" were typified by this

Table 1. Obstacles to Including Public Archaeology/Cultural Resource Management in Curriculum.

(respondents could choose multiple answers)

Type of Program	Lack of faculty training		Lack of faculty interest		Lack of student interest		Other courses take priority		Inappropriate in our academic setting	
Undergraduate only (N=60)	28	42%	25	42%	18	30%	37	62%	24	40%
Graduate & undergraduate (N=57)	28	49%	35	61%	23	40%	35	61%	18	32%

one from a large, prestigious department at a private research university. "Our program has a strong orientation toward anthropological theory. One can't do everything, so we leave cultural resource management to those who do it well."

Another set of questions included in the questionnaire attempted to assess the makeup of the student population in archaeology. Statistics on the population of Ph.D. recipients are gathered by the AAA, and the Department of Education collects statistics about all students in larger categories like "social sciences," but there is a dearth of reporting on archaeology students. These figures are not "hard data" in the sense of official records from registrars or the like. About 80 percent of the responses were "estimates" and only 20 percent "actual" counts, but there is enough information here to reinforce the common impression of a profession made up of, and teaching to, a very white population of students.

Of the 117 departments returning the survey form, 107 gave information on how graduates of their programs fit into the census categories used by the U.S. government to classify people by race or ethnic background. We asked for this information about their graduates during the past 4 years (1994 through 1997).

The proportion of minority to white graduates is enormously skewed. The departments reported a total of 5,402 graduates (these figures combine actual counts and estimates), of which 4,626 (86 percent) were White, 320 (6 percent) Hispanic, 187 (3 percent) Asian, 161 (3 percent) Black, 82 (2 percent) Native American or Alaskan, and 26 (1 percent) Hawaiian.

Fourteen institutions (13 percent) reported no minority graduates at all; and only one reported no White graduates. Of the departments reporting graduates in more than one non-White category, 43 (40 percent) reported graduates in 1 or 2 categories, and 50 (47 percent) reported graduates in 3 or more categories (Table 2).

Only 6 departments reported graduating 20 or more minority

Table 2. Institutions Reporting Minority Graduates.

Census category	Number of institutions reporting graduates	Percentage of institutions reporting graduates
White	106	99%
Hispanic	71	66%
Black	60	5%
Asian or Pacific Islander	49	46%
American Indian or Native Alaskan	44	41%
Hawaiian	13	12%

students (all categories) in the 4 years between 1994 and 1997. Because this number is so small, it was impossible to identify any common elements among these more diversified departments. Another caution is that figures for "your program," were requested and it is not known if the respondents reported archaeology graduates or graduates in all subfields in their departments. If they did include graduates in subjects or subfields in addition to archaeology, the results are even more discouraging.

To provide a better sense of the reliability of these data, the types of departments responding were reviewed. Departments of anthropology represented 61 percent of the responses while departments of anthropology combined with one or two other departments/programs accounted for 27 percent. The remaining 12 percent came from various other departments and programs. In addition, the majority of responses came from departments with over 11 faculty members. On the one hand, the survey includes most of the kinds of institutions of higher learning in which archaeology is taught. On the other, because it is based on departments listed in the AAA *Guide*, it is probably biased in favor of larger and more comprehensive departments, and more selective institutions. As such, it seriously overlooks community colleges, historically Black colleges, tribal colleges, and small liberal arts institutions—both public and private.

The list of responding departments was compared to a composite of several lists published in the January *Anthropology Newsletter* as part of an article discussing the value of "best department" lists (Evans 1998). Despite the fact that the gist of that article was that any single list was apt to be incomplete and misleading, it was interesting to see how many of all the departments so identified were included in our data. The composite list totaled 45 departments, and 15 of them had returned questionnaires to us. Since this is roughly in proportion to the total response to the total mailing (117 of 343 departments responding), it appears that the returns were on target.

The picture of the current status of teaching public archaeology/

cultural resource management in higher education that is emerging is that departments are offering these subjects in a variety of formats that vary with the size and nature of their programs. More encouragingly, we see that twice as many departments are currently planning to add specific courses in these topics than are now offering them. The problem remains, however, that more than half of all departments are quick to say that teaching public archaeology/cultural resource management is not a high priority, indicating that they still make a distinction between "public archaeology" and "real archaeology." In addition, there is the question of the departments that did not respond to the survey. Finally there is the overarching question with which we must wrestle: can we communicate effectively with diverse publics if we are not a diverse profession?

Student Survey

SAA asked the Student Affairs Committee to solicit information from students regarding public archaeology and cultural resource management training and education. Students were asked to respond to the following questions:

1) What university or college do you currently attend?
2) What type of employment are you preparing for?
3) What type of job do you expect to get after graduation? Indicate your degree level.
4) Are you getting the courses and training you need for those jobs?
5) Do you see a need for Ph.D. programs in applied archaeology that would prepare archaeologists for jobs in public archaeology/cultural resource management?

Forty-nine students from 16 academic institutions responded to SAA's information request. Although this is a small sample, some general statements are possible. The vast majority—63.3 percent (31)—of the students reported that they were preparing for jobs as university professors while 28.6 percent (14) reported that they were working towards employment in governmental or private cultural resource management positions. A few (8.2 percent, or 4) hedged their bets by preparing for both (not a bad move given today's job market). When asked what type of job they expected, the numbers were the same—e.g., students felt that they were preparing for the types of jobs they would eventually obtain. The high percentage of students indicating they were preparing for academic positions is not surprising, as 71.5 percent (35) indicated that they were currently enrolled in Ph.D. programs. Not surprisingly, the percent of M.A. degree candidates (24.5 percent, or 12) and the percent preparing for jobs in cultural resource management (28.6 percent, or 14) were consistent.

Regardless of the degree being pursued, 88.8 percent (42) felt that they were receiving the training they needed for the jobs they hoped to obtain. All those in Ph.D. programs preparing for academic positions felt they were getting the training they needed. However, all 8 (16.4 percent) responses indicating that they were not getting the education and training they needed were M.A. candidates preparing for cultural resource management employment or Ph.D. candidates preparing for both academic and cultural resource management positions. Given that the majority of the respondents were preparing for academic positions, it is interesting to note that 61.3 percent (30) saw the need for an applied archaeology program that would prepare students not only as academic archaeologists but for jobs in public archaeology and cultural resource management.

Students provided some interesting comments regarding public archaeology and cultural resource management. There were a number of students who felt that such education and training need only be provided at the M.A. level for those entering public archaeology and cultural resource management, while several others noted that there were few academic positions for doctoral-level archaeologists and that in fact many would likely find employment in applied areas of archaeology. However, optimism was expressed by one student who said, "Somebody's getting academic jobs; why not me?" while another student said, "Getting an academic teaching position was like winning the lottery." The majority of the students said that education and training in these areas should not exist as a separate track because they felt that it would further fracture the discipline and that students pursuing these types of careers must take courses in method and theory as well.

In addition, students felt that criteria should be established for the kinds of information and courses that should be available to students interested in public archaeology and cultural resource management. As one student put it, "Applied work should have a theoretical component and theoretical works should be practical." A number of students indicated that some of these types of courses, especially ethics, and grant and proposal writing, should be required for all students regardless of job expectations. Concern was expressed that archaeologists educating and training students at academic institutions needed to meet with archaeologists in applied areas to discuss common concerns and issues relating to public archaeology and cultural resource management. As stated by one student, "...The rich diversity of experiences these two orientations in archaeology share could be mutually beneficial to the practitioners as well as the students." There was concern that archaeology can be a business but that it should not be turned into one. One student expressed the concern that having a Ph.D. from an applied program might make it difficult to "sell" oneself as a teacher.

Overall, the student respondents to the survey were aware that the vast majority of them would not find employment as university professors and that they would, at least during some part of their careers, find employment in public archaeology and cultural resource management in the private and/or governmental sectors. Yet, at the same time, most of them indicated that they were preparing for and seeking academic positions. With few exceptions, they felt that courses or components within an existing course in public archaeology and cultural resource management would be beneficial. There was a strong concern that public archaeology and cultural resource management not exist as a separate degree track but as a component of both undergraduate and graduate education leading to a degree in anthropology. For the most part, they said, such education and training was was being omitted from present-day anthropology programs.

References Cited

American Anthropological Association
  1997   *Guide: A Guide to Programs, A Directory of Members.* American Anthropological Association, Arlington, Virginia.

Evans, P.
  1998   Evaluating Academic Departments from the Outside. In *Anthropology Newsletter* 39(1):22ff.

II.
A Proposal to Guide Curricular Reform for the Twenty-First Century

A Proposal to Guide Curricular Reform for the Twenty-First Century

edited by Susan J. Bender [1]

The basic premise informing this approach to curricular reform is that how we teach archaeology is no longer consistent with how we practice archaeology in the early twenty-first century. Position papers prepared by participants for the Wakulla Springs workshop mentioned this point time and again, as have a number of other collectives within the profession whose recommendations eventually coalesced in the workshop (see Bender and Smith 1998). The task in crafting a proposal for reform was thus not to agree that something needed to change or why even such change was needed; rather, it was to reach consensus on the content of such change. The subsequent section in this volume, "Framing Discussions: Considering the Contexts," details participants' individual perspectives on the implications of significant changes in archaeological practice and clarifies some of this debate as collectively we sought to determine how these changes should direct curricular reform. A few general statements here on that debate can fashion a conceptual framework for this section and present a general proposal for curricular reform. The emphasis here is on the word "proposal," with the expectation that it will be discussed and modified as these ideas are debated by the profession (see final "Discussion" section).

For a number of participants in the Wakulla Springs workshop, the central issue propelling curricular reform was how to train our students more appropriately for the range of career opportunities that await them after graduate school. For others, the key issue centered on teaching all our students that archaeology is practiced and learned within a public setting—a setting which profoundly affects our pursuit of knowledge about the past. A number of participants also debated whether archaeology still had significant and meaningful ties to the rest of anthropology, ties that would warrant the teaching of archaeology within the context of an anthropological education. In the end, we reached consensus that the following statement captured our sense of the range of issues to which curricular reform should respond, where order of listing does not necessarily reflect priority. In it we have attempted to identify the specific contexts that have significantly altered archaeological practice and thus require that we rethink our approach to educating our students.

During the past two decades, archaeological practice has been transformed by forces both internal and external to the

profession. These transformations include a growth of the
market in antiquities accompanied by unprecedented site
destruction; the threatening of our archaeological heritage
by construction and development activities; the implementation of cultural resource legislation and the subsequent
growth of the cultural resource management profession; the
passage of legislation regulating access to human burials and
artifact collections; heightened popular interest in archaeology, including the growing interest of descendant communities in their archaeological pasts; and the equal effects of
these factors on prehistoric and historic archaeology such
that distinctions between the two have become blurred.

We agreed that these forces have required archaeologists to develop new skills and ethical principles for professional practice and that contemporary curricula frequently overlook the need to teach about these.
The goal of our reform proposal must thus be to identify the relevant
skills and principles and to suggest how they might be woven into undergraduate, graduate, and professional development curricula. Having
reached consensus on these issues, we quickly recognized that SAA's
Principles of Archaeological Ethics both describes the ethical implications
of these forces and articulates the skills required for applying the principles in practice. Hence this statement provided inspiration for a number of
our proposed principles for reform. At the same time, ever mindful of the
resonance between the skills and principles being advocated and traditional liberal arts values, we sought to emphasize this complementary
aspect. The following set of principles derives from these joint concerns.

Principles for Curricular Reform

• *Stewardship*. An archaeology curriculum should foster stewardship by teaching students that archaeological resources are nonrenewable
and finite and must have complete and substantial documentation.

• *Diverse Pasts*. An archaeology curriculum should make students
aware that archaeologists no longer have exclusive rights to the interpretation of archaeological resources, but that various publics have a stake in
the past. Diverse groups—such as descendant communities; state, local,
and federal agencies; and others—compete for and have vested interests
in the nonrenewable resources of the past. Teaching students to negotiate
the complexities of participation in a diverse society is increasingly articulated as a goal of a liberal arts education.

• *Social Relevance*. If archaeology is to be justified as a discipline
in terms of both public support and interest, then we must effectively
articulate the ways in which we can use the past to help students think
productively about the present and future.

• *Ethics and Values*. The articulation of ethics and values are seen as the sign of growth and maturation in the profession. The eight SAA Principles of Archaeological Ethics are fundamental to how archaeologists should conduct themselves with regard to archaeological resources, data, colleagues, and the public. The linkage of these principles to specific points within the curriculum will provide students with a basic foundation for the study of cultural resources, as well as promote a traditional goal of liberal arts education: values clarification.

• *Written and Oral Communication.* Archaeology depends on the understanding and support of the public. For this to occur, archaeologists must be able to communicate their goals, results, and recommendations to diverse audiences. This goal must be supported by teaching our students how to think logically, write effectively, and speak clearly, all of which are central aims of a liberal arts education.

• *Fundamental Archaeological Skills.* Students planning a career in archaeology must have mastered a set of basic cognitive and methodological skills that will enable them to operate effectively in field and laboratory contexts. These skills must include excavation, analysis, report writing, and long-term curation.

• *Real-World Problem Solving.* Effective learning can be significantly enhanced by asking students to engage in problem-solving work. Such work can be accomplished either through case studies in a classroom context or internship experience. In either case, students are asked to apply the knowledge and skills articulated above in the solution of a fully contextualized archaeological problem.

Curricular reform should proceed through consideration of how these principles can be integrated into existing course structures at all levels of the curriculum. We envision that such work will result in curricula with traditional course structure and content that are significantly enhanced by the introduction of topics implied by the principles. The vehicles for the introduction of such topics are likely to be more diverse readings and assignments and pedagogical strategies than all new courses and course sequences. Suggestions for the implementation of such reform in undergraduate, graduate, and professional development programs are outlined below.

Undergraduate Education

The undergraduate curriculum accommodates a diverse array of students with widely varying levels of interest in archaeology. Potential reformers must take these differences into account and make thoughtful decisions about the principles most appropriate for the introductory level and those best suited for more advanced students pursuing a deeper understanding of the discipline.

The implications of the above principles for the undergraduate curriculum are discussed below. A table summarizes the articulation among standard undergraduate courses, the audiences typically encountered in them, and the reform principles most appropriate to both (see page 38). The approach suggested by this schema is, of course, only one of many possibilities; we recognize that a variety of alterations to it may be warranted for any particular undergraduate program.

Stewardship

In considering archaeological resources, students need to understand the nonrenewable nature of archaeological sites and associated material. Students should be able to articulate the information content of such material and the value of the data in interpreting and understanding human behavior. Once the information has been removed from the ground, whether through archaeological excavation or as a result of looting, development, erosion, or other processes, the site itself is gone. In the case of archaeological investigations, the material from the ground is transformed into data in the form of collections, records, and reports that are used to interpret and explain the past.

As part of this discussion, students should come to comprehend the damage caused by looting sites and trafficking artifacts in the form of information and interpretation loss. Examples of looted sites such as Slack Farms or the impact of vandalism on many sites in the Southwest can be discussed. Students can evaluate the loss of information that has occurred as a result of these actions in terms of what we might have, but now never will, learn about these sites and the people who once occupied them.

A third part of the discussion should focus on explaining the conservation ethic—i.e., how the past can be preserved. Once students understand the value of archaeological resources and their fragile nature, they need to examine methods of conservation. Conservation, or the wise use of resources, can include stabilizing an archaeological site, preserving it in place, excavating, or fostering public understanding of the information content of the resources through site development and interpretation. Examples of sites that have been the focus of conservation methods can be discussed (e.g., those developed sites such as Cahokia or Mesa Verde; ongoing site interpretation such as in Alexandria, Va.; site protection through Site Stewards). In addition, it should be noted that the movement toward conservation has boosted the employment of archaeologists as cultural resource managers. This segment of the profession, now comprising at least half of all employed archaeologists, emphasizes stewardship of the archaeological record. As part of this responsibility, archaeologists now work with many different publics to communicate the value and importance of archaeological data. In more advanced courses, this discussion should include a review of preservation laws such as the Archaeological Resources Protection Act, National Historic Preservation Act, and Native

American Graves Protection and Repatriation Act. Comparison of these laws with similar legislation in other countries also is relevant to these considerations.

Diverse Interests

Undergraduate students in archaeology courses should come to understand that archaeologists no longer have exclusive rights to the past, but that various publics have a stake in it. No one truly "owns" the past; rather, we all share common roots in a past that bears different fruits. Those groups that compete for and have vested interests in the nonrenewable resources of the past include descendant communities; state, local, and federal agencies; and others (e.g., salvers, "metal detectors"). Junior-or senior-level undergraduates should learn how the development of partnerships with these diverse groups can be used to enhance mutual understanding and deepen our interpretations of the past. Moreover, students need to learn about basic preservation laws to gain perspective on the profession's commitment to the protection of our common heritage. Finally, through examination of the ways that the products of the past have been used to further political and national interests, students should become aware of the social implications of our discipline. By recognizing that our differing views rise from common roots, we can understand the relationships we share, extend our influence beyond our individual reach, and unite to attain our common goals.

Social Relevance

In the past, archaeologists have considered the social benefits of their inquiry to be self-evident. Teachers simply presented the "substance" of the discipline and assumed that students would intuitively see its value. But this complacent view can no longer govern the way that archaeology is taught. Those of us who teach archaeology in the twenty-first century must convey to our students why *we* believe that archaeology is important in response to the claims of diverse and competing interest groups.

One way to convey archaeology's relevance to today's students is to highlight ways in which we can use the past to help us think productively about the present and the future. As we teach archaeology, particularly in introductory and large-enrollment courses, it is essential that we show our students how understandings gained from archaeology may be relevant to the issues we face today. For convenience, we may call this approach "Lessons from the Past." Here are some examples:

• Discussing the role of environment on the development of past societies, including the effects of environmental degradation.

• Discussing the history and role of warfare in relation to politics, economy, and other historical circumstances.

- Discussing the history of cities and urban life, and the many forms these took in the past.

- Discussing how archaeological techniques can be applied directly in matters of public policy and the law, such as in the case of forensic studies (Bosnia) and the University of Arizona's "Garbage Project."

- Discussing past systems of social inequality, and drawing connections to and contrasts with the present.

- Discussing the history of human health and disease.

Professional Ethics and Values

Undergraduate students should be familiar with the eight SAA Principles of Archaeological Practice and come to understand that they are fundamental to how archaeologists conduct themselves in relation to the resources, their data, their colleagues, and the public. These principles should be linked to specific lecture topics, or treated in individual lectures to provide advanced undergraduates with a basic foundation upon which to establish their interest in the study of cultural resources. The Code of Ethics and Standards of Research Performance of the Register of Professional Archaeologists are a more detailed set of ethical behaviors relative to the specific practice of research. Since these statements provide direction and foundation for the practice of field archaeology and its consequences, they should be incorporated into discussions and assignments in upper-division courses.

Communication

Archaeologists must be able to communicate their goals, results, and recommendations clearly and effectively to a variety of publics. Acquiring the skills to do so should begin in the undergraduate classroom. Written and oral presentations that require logical thinking and argumentation need to be a common feature of coursework, and the complexity of these assignments should increase through upper-division courses. At least some of this work should be aimed at communication with nonspecialist audiences, so that students learn how to communicate their ideas without relying on jargon or other forms of specialized communication that inhibit public understanding of archaeology. Effective communication also includes mastery of standard presentation tools like computers and the Internet, as well as the ability to interact cooperatively and effectively with others involved in creating a product or reaching a decision.

Basic Archaeological Skills

Students planning a career in archaeology need to have mastered a set of basic skills. At a conceptual level, students must be able to make pertinent observations of the archaeological record, record and describe these observations, and draw appropriate inferences. The technical skills that students should control include basic principles of surveying and cartography (e.g., map making and reading), stratigraphy (e.g., ability to draw accurately and interpret a soil profile), archaeological methods (e.g., ability to complete field and laboratory forms), database management (e.g., ability to create and use data tables), and technical writing (e.g., ability to write artifact, feature, and site descriptions). Upper-division courses need to ensure that students graduating with a specialization in archaeology acquire these skills.

Real-World Problem Solving

One of the most difficult things for undergraduates to do is to connect the classroom and the real world. In the realm of coursework, helping students make this connection often involves emphasizing main points and demonstrating applicability to their lives and professions. "Real-world problem solving" means flexibility and grounding in the basics of archaeology. Students can be engaged in problem solving through classroom examples or observations of real situations. An important aspect of reality is communicating that archaeology is one of *many* interests that must be reconciled to complete a project successfully. Having students attend a session or meeting of a descendant population where archaeology is discussed would be an eye-opener.

In addition, it is our public service responsibility as professors of archaeology to demonstrate through examples and assignments how business, politics, and local communities or bureaucracies interact in dispute resolution. Archaeology outside the academy is usually done to help resolve a problem in construction and development or a disputed location of something, or as part of a plan to avoid a future problem. Students can experience this process by attending a routine local city or county commission meeting or listening to a politician lecture to the class about the political process. All of this work should be accomplished in the context of student learning about the impact of preservation law and regulations.

Embedding the Principles in Existing Curricula

Curricula can be revised effectively and efficiently simply by embedding the reform principles in existing course structures. To assist in planning revision of this type, standard undergraduate courses and their audiences (target students) are identified and matched in Table 1, along with information on which ethical principles can or should be introduced in which course contexts. Suggestions then follow for specific topics appropriate for teaching each principle to particular target audiences.

Table 1. Cross-tabulation of Standard Undergraduate Courses, Principles Appropriate for Introduction in Each Course, and Target Student Audiences.

	Stewardship	Diverse Interests	Social Relevance	Professional Ethics & Values	Communication	Basic Archaeological Skills	Real-World Problem Solving	Target Students [a]
Introductory Anthropology	X							1,2
Introductory Courses	X							1,2,3
• Cultural Anthropology								
• Archaeology								
• Bioanthropology								
• Linguistics								
World Archaeology	X	X	X					1,2,3
Area Archaeology	X	X	X					1,2,3
Archaeological Methods and Theory	X	X		X	X	X	X	1,2,3
Principles of Archaeology	X	X		X	X		X	2,3
Archaeological Field School		X		X	X	X	X	3
Archaeological Laboratory Methods				X	X	X		3
Internships				X	X	X	X	3

[a] 1. Non-majors (1 course); 2. Anthropology Majors (who enter another profession); 3. Archaeology Track Majors (who attend graduate school in archaeology)

Suggested Topics:

Stewardship
Looters and Trafficking
Conservation Ethic
Nonrenewable Resource

Diverse Interests
Different Views of Past
Partnerships (collaboration with many groups)
Public Involvement (reporting results)
Politics Uses of the Past (nation building)

Social Relevance (lessons from the past)
Garbage
Population Dynamics
Environmental History
Systems of Social Inequality
Warfare
Health/Disease

Professional Ethics and Values
Principles of Archaeological Ethics
Preservation Law

Communication
Clear writing (implied clear thinking)
Clear speaking (implied clear thinking)
Public Speaking
Computer Literacy

Basic Archaeological Skills
Observations skill (inferential skills)
Basic map skills (scales, contours)
Organize and assess data
Knowledge of the law
Description (one step above field description)

Real-World Problem Solving
Professional Responsibilities and Accountability
Archaeopolitics (know the players and process)
Citizenship (civics)
How business works
Legal and regulatory (know the rules)

Graduate Education

It is tempting to think of graduate education as a process that
results in the production of Ph.D.s. However, as in the case of undergrad-

uate education, we must retain a sense of the diversity of students that actually enroll in graduate archaeology programs. Many practicing archaeologists complete their degree work at the M.A. level, and these future professionals represent a substantial percentage of students in any given graduate archaeology course. Moreover, archaeologists who complete their graduate work at the M.A. level in particular have a substantial impact on archaeological resources and their management, as well on opinions of the profession held by various public audiences. Our recommendations for reform in graduate education therefore represent our vision of the essential standards in knowledge, skills, and abilities for practice in historic and prehistoric archaeology.

We are mindful that some doctoral programs do not build upon master's degree programs and might not even provide for granting the M.A. degree during the course of doctoral study. We believe that in these cases the earlier portion of the doctoral program should be enhanced along the lines recommended here for master's degree programs. We note that those seeking doctoral training and careers as professors at research universities will inevitably be called upon to provide instruction to students whose own careers will require the elements we regard as essential in a graduate program.

There is strong sentiment that students should demonstrate competency in research and writing through the completion of an M.A. thesis, Ph.D. dissertation, or an equivalent project. Successful completion of these original research projects demonstrate that a student is prepared to conduct independent research, participate in the management of significant archaeological resources, and evaluate the research and contributions of colleagues and peers.

It is imperative that students receive instruction and training on ethics and professionalism in archaeology throughout the graduate program. Discussion of ethical principles, codes, and policies as published by the Archaeological Institute of America (AIA); Archeology Division, American Anthropological Association (AAA); Canadian Archaeology Association (CAA); Society for American Archaeology (SAA); Society for Historical Archaeology (SHA); and Society of Professional Archaeologists/Register of Professional Archaeologists (SOPA/The Register) should be incorporated into coursework wherever possible. This training should convey the finite and nonrenewable nature of archaeological resources and the threat to archaeological resources from development and the illegal antiquities trade. Graduate training in archaeology should emphasize the stewardship responsibility of professional archaeologists as identified in the Principles of Archaeological Ethics of the Society for American Archaeology as well as those of other professional societies.

Undergraduate Prerequisites

These central requirements for graduate study clearly build on foundations in writing and other forms of communication developed in the undergraduate curriculum, and assume that students enter graduate study with a well-developed understanding of archaeology as professional practice. The latter element of undergraduate training can be achieved through implementing recommendations included under the "Stewardship," "Professional Ethics," and "Real-World Problem Solving" principles discussed above. In addition, students should enter graduate programs with an understanding of the relationship between research methods and archaeological theory. This goal can be achieved in upper-division courses that substantively engage students in both laboratory and fieldwork as described in the "Basic Archaeological Skills" principle discussed in the preceding section.

We also recommend that students enter graduate programs with a knowledge base that extends the central undergraduate training described in the principles for reform. We believe such understanding to be essentially supportive of graduate-level research, with a recognition of archaeology's essential connections to anthropology. Before entering a graduate program, students must develop a strong, well-rounded background in anthropology with coursework in archaeology, cultural anthropology, and biological anthropology. Training in these subfields of anthropology is essential background for a graduate program specialization in archaeology. As part of this preparation, students should take at least one course that specializes in the archaeology of a particular area or region. Familiarity with North American archaeology is especially desirable, since this knowledge is required in many federal employment venues and is useful for students planning to pursue careers in cultural resource management. Finally, undergraduate students should develop competency in at least one foreign language which may be useful in researching at the graduate level and in developing an appreciation for cultural diversity.

Graduate Core Competencies

The following list identifies essential knowledge and skill sets required of practicing archaeologists. As is appropriate for professional track study, these recommendations focus primarily on developing research-level knowledge and skills. Note, however, that reform principles dealing with "Ethics," "Real-World Problem Solving," "Stewardship," and "Diverse Interests" are represented in several of the graduate-level skill and knowledge sets, including "Ethics, Law, and Professionalism"; "Broad-based Field Experience"; and "Cultural Resource Management and Preservation." Finally, we believe that students' ability to interpret the past is enhanced by deepening their understanding of the implications of the anthropological perspective for their work.

A Core Course (Other than Archaeology) in One of the Subdisciplines of Anthropology. Programs may require more than one core course in the subdisciplines of anthropology, but a minimum of one is required to maintain an understanding of archaeology's role in anthropology.

Ethics, Law, and Professionalism. Formal training in laws and government regulations that pertain to archaeology is essential and should be taught in association with archaeological ethics. Courses should provide students with an introduction to the ethical issues that face the archaeological profession, and an understanding between ethical and legal conduct. The purpose of the course should be to develop an understanding of professionalism among archaeology students, and introduce students to the types of "real-world" problem solving which is now often associated with all aspects of archaeology.

Method and Theory. Graduate students should complete advanced coursework in archaeological method and theory. Students should receive formal training in development of research designs, hypothesis testing, data collection, and so on. This training is intended to provide students with a basis for designing their own research and evaluating the research of colleagues.

Statistics. All graduate students in archaeology must develop an understanding of quantitative methods and the use of statistics in archaeological research. This represent a basic skill needed for archaeological research.

Supervised, Broad-based Field Experience. It is essential that all graduate students participate in formally supervised field research that teaches them basic skills (e.g., mapping, photography, survey, sampling, data recording, and record keeping). Through this experience, students should comprehend the nonrenewable nature of archaeological resources and the destructive nature of archaeological research. The fieldwork experience also should encourage students to construct their work as problem-oriented research that selects only those methods that use that portion of the archaeological record needed to solve the research problem. Students also should learn to apply nondestructive research techniques like geophysical surveys (e.g., magnetometer, soil resistance meter, soil conductivity meter, ground-penetrating radar) to encourage the conservation ethic as integral to their field training.

Survey Course of Archaeological Sciences. Students should receive formal instruction in application of non-archaeological sciences to the study of archaeological resources and research problems. Basic training in a wide range of possible research areas, including but not limited to faunal and floral analysis, soils and stratigraphic analysis, geophysical survey methods, archaeological dating techniques, skeletal and isotope analysis of human bones, and ceramic compositional analysis, should be a central part of a graduate student's skill and knowledge base.

Cultural Resource Management and Preservation. The management and study of archaeological resources as mandated by law and regulations has become a major part of archaeology. Students should be exposed to the contemporary practice of cultural resource management through case studies or internship experience associated with "real-world problem solving."

Statement Regarding the Ph.D. Degree

The Ph.D. degree is an advanced graduate degree that recognizes specialized research achievement beyond the master's level. We anticipate that doctoral programs will continue to expect students to take additional courses in subjects such as statistics and specialized seminars, and master an additional language or research skill. Ph.D. programs should be structured to recognize the special expertise in oral and written communication skills required by educators and the directors of research projects with high visibility. Thus, we envision that the Ph.D. provides for the enhanced training in the aforementioned areas as well as a specific research focus. The Ph.D. must continue to involve production of a doctoral dissertation, which might in some circumstances obviate the need for a master's thesis at an earlier stage of graduate study.

Professional Development

The rapidly changing sociopolitical and technological contexts for archaeological practice not only require that we update how we teach our students, they also demand that we identify and develop opportunities for professional archaeologists to refine, maintain, and update their knowledge and skills. To encourage all practicing archaeologists to see themselves as lifelong learners, the professional societies must promote through various incentives the participation of their members in continuing education opportunities. These opportunities may include courses, workshops, plenary and other sessions at Annual Meetings, publications, and guides to resources. The professional development opportunities should be rigorous and continually evaluated and updated to be consistent with the guidelines offered by the ethical principles and "best practices" identified by the discipline. In other words, the reform principles as articulated here can and should be made applicable to the professional development needs of all professional archaeologists. In the following section, several recommendations are made on how this newly conceived aspect of archaeology education might be implemented within a framework consistent with our goals for undergraduate and graduate education.

Formats for Ongoing Professional Development

All practicing archaeologists should have access to continuing education opportunities. The target audience includes archaeological technicians, archaeology educators, cultural resource managers, contract archaeologists, public interpreters, and teaching faculty, as well as professionals in related fields of research, teaching, decision making and resource management. Professionals in diverse work settings require access to continuing studies opportunities in a variety of formats including courses, workshops, symposia, online seminars, moderated listservs, resource guides, case studies, and publications. Development of the resources to meet these needs will require the participation of many educational institutions and professional organizations, especially those willing to take an entrepreneurial approach.

Some preliminary steps to facilitate the development of continuing education opportunities can be taken. These include compiling information on existing workshops; classes; and educational resources including publications, Websites, and videos; and evaluating their appropriateness for professional development. Another step is the identification of mechanisms to deliver professional development opportunities via collaborative efforts involving professional societies such as SAA, SHA, AIA, SOPA/the Register, and credit-giving institutions. The executive boards of professional societies and organizers of conferences and meetings should be enlisted to encourage participation in these learning opportunities.

Access to resource materials is an important component of professional development. This includes both dissemination of information about existing materials and development of new resources. Cultural resource management texts, collections of case studies, online syntheses of federal regulations, and a source book for archaeology—a sort of "Whole Earth" catalog for archaeologists—are among the types of materials that need to be developed in support of professional development. Current issues in such areas as ethnography, public education, and sociopolitics could be addressed in a series of booklets or pamphlets, as well as through regular electronic communication. Increased access to unpublished reports and other "gray" literature should be promoted on a state-by-state basis, with online availability of the bibliographies of technical titles as a first step.

Principles of Archaeological Ethics as a Framework for Learning
While the potential audience for professional development is broad and the formats are multiple, SAA's Principles of Archaeological Ethics can provide a unifying set of themes for postgraduate education, just as they did for undergraduate and graduate curricular reform. Concepts of stewardship and conservation, effective communication with diverse public audiences, and maintenance of high levels of basic archaeological knowledge and skills are centrally embedded in the themes of stewardship, accountability, commercialization, public education and outreach, intellectual property, public reporting and publication, records and preservation,

and training and resources. The following points state the core concept of each principle and list examples of relevant professional development needs and opportunities.

Principle No. 1: Stewardship. All archaeologists must work for the long-term conservation and protection of the irreplaceable archaeological record by practicing and promoting stewardship.

The overarching stewardship principle should be supported by a broadly defined set of continuing education opportunities that enhance archaeologists' abilities to promote widespread participation in preservation issues by the public and professionals alike. These should address archaeological ethics, law, and professionalism in a manner similar to that discussed in the "graduate core competencies" above. Laws should be addressed on both a national and a state-by-state basis, including providing accessible and updated information about laws and compliance issues, as well as state-based workshops on laws for target audiences, including contractors, resource managers, and archaeologists.

Within our professional societies, the overarching quality of the stewardship principle can be recognized through support of plenary sessions and forums that address its theoretical and applied implications. As part of the profession's ongoing reflection and development in light of the principle, thesis and dissertation research based on archival collections rather than excavation should be encouraged. Workshops and other training sessions to facilitate the conduct and supervision of such research are highly recommended.

Principle No. 2: Accountability. Responsible archaeological research requires public accountability and active consultation with affected groups.

Seminars on partnerships, lobbying, and consultation practices might address advocacy with politicians, developers, and others controlling and affecting the archaeological resource base. Relationships with descendant and affected communities should be addressed in relation to theoretical contexts of project design as well as all aspects of communication and consultation. Workshops and interactive courses on conflict resolution, management skills, and human relations should be developed and promoted.

Principle No. 3: Commercialization. Archaeologists should discourage and avoid activities that enhance the commercial value of archaeological objects and contribute to site destruction.

There is a general need for access to case studies and information on looting and prosecutions related to the archaeological record. Short courses on international laws and agreements and ethical issues related to the antiquities trade, museum and private collections, and specialized areas such as shipwrecks would be valuable. Continuing education also should address popular images and public perceptions of archaeology as a treasure hunt.

Principle No. 4: Public Education and Outreach. Archaeologists should participate in cooperative efforts with others to improve the preservation and interpretation of the record by enlisting public support and communicating interpretations of the past.

Training to improve communication skills, including technical and popular writing, is an important area to address through workshops, distance learning, and writing guides with examples. Working with the media includes developing skills in producing a media kit and discussing complex issues in clear and simple language.

Emphasis should continue to be placed on working with K-12 teachers and other educators. Information about existing resource lists, resource exhibits, and workshops at Annual Meetings should be widely disseminated and targeted to all archaeological professionals. Federal and state agencies and other organizations with public education programs, including museums and parks, should be encouraged to enhance their outreach to archaeologists in all areas of the profession.

Principle No. 5: Intellectual Property. The knowledge and documents created through the study of archaeological resources are part of the archaeological record and must be made available to others within a reasonable time.

Among the continuing education needs in this area is the availability of case studies to illustrate the need for this principle. Relevant formative literature might include guides to the proper use of archaeological archives and databases, copyright laws, and proper citations, including electronic formats. Guidelines for proper paper presentations, the ethics of interaction with descendant communities, and formal professional courtesy would make valuable contributions to the continuing education of professional archaeologists.

Principle No. 6: Public Reporting and Publication. Archaeologists must present knowledge gained from investigation of the archaeological record to interested publics in timely and accessible forms.

Topics for workshops and guides include technical writing with clarity, ethical issues in public presentation of archaeological information, and the development of programs, displays, and popular publications from technical information. Professional development in this area relates closely to Principle No. 4: Public Education and Outreach.

Principle No. 7: Records and Preservation. Archaeologists should work actively for the preservation, responsible use, and accessibility of archaeological collections, records, and reports.

Professional development must pay attention to the need for effective curation and management of archaeological collections and records. Supportive resource materials include technical guides and bibliographies and case studies of good and bad collection management practices. Efforts should be directed at raising awareness of these concerns and developing strategies for preserving the records and reports of archaeologists who retire or leave the profession.

Principle No. 8: Training and Resources. Archaeologists must have adequate training, experience, facilities, and other support necessary to conduct research in accordance with the foregoing principles.

Continuing studies offerings must provide opportunities to gain specialized training or expertise related to job responsibilities. They should also address changes in laws, technologies and archaeological best practices. Maintaining the expectation of staying up-to-date in these areas, and having the means to do it are as important for the professor of under-graduate and graduate students as for the field archaeologist and lab technician.

Finally, self-evaluation provides an excellent strategy for activating these principles in our professional practice. This process would include writing a personal mission statement *vis a vis* the Principles of Archaeological Ethics and documenting one's professional skills through resume writing. This self-reflection should be mirrored by a protocol for evaluation of the workplace. A model of such evaluation might be developed and presented via newsletters, bulletins, or sessions at Annual Meetings.

Conclusion

Although the proposal outlined above will trigger considerable debate across the profession, it does capture in substantive ways our need to reform and redefine the goals of archaeology curricula at all levels of interest and expertise. Since the need to undertake such revision is driven largely by the changing contexts for archaeological practice, these have been defined and utilized as a framework for the proposal. The SAA Principles of Archaeological Ethics provide an overarching structure for this effort, since they articulate professional training and practice in sub-stantive ways by their sociopolitical, technical, intellectual, and employment contexts. Moreover, this proposal recognizes a diversity of student interest and expertise in archaeology education but still focuses on common educational goals. Instruction in archaeology as a discipline that fosters stewardship of a shared, yet contested resource base; seeks to create new knowledge about the past via increasingly sophisticated technical applications; is regulated in large part by law; and articulates its findings to a wide range of public audiences is the framework that shapes these recommendations for undergraduate, graduate, and professional development curricula.

The review of this proposal by the profession will inevitably strengthen it while retaining its central features. In the end, it is the hope of this publication's contributors to stimulate sufficient change in the content and pedagogies of archaeology education to create a discipline-wide sense that the learning goals of any course or course sequence need to serve the interests of our students and our profession in specific ways. At the most basic level, students who take only one course in archaeology should take away from that experience an appreciation for the value and fragility of archaeological resources. At the other end of the continuum, we seek to develop a wide range of educational opportunities for all professional archaeologists as a way to keep them abreast of new research and teaching strategies and technologies, as well as of changing laws and best practices in the field. Our ultimate aim is to inspire curricular reform that will result in cohorts of students who are truly educated in the goals and means of contemporary archaeological practice.

Notes

[1] This section was developed from reports appearing in the *SAA Bulletin* [Susan J. Bender & George S. Smith, November 1998, "SAA's Workshop on Teaching Archaeology in the 21st Century: Promoting a National Dialogue on Curricula Reform," *SAA Bulletin* 16(5): 11-13; Hester A. Davis et al., January 1999, "Teaching Archaeology in the 21st Century: Thoughts on Undergraduate Education," *SAA Bulletin* 17(1): 18-20, 22; Mark J. Lynott et al., January 1999, "Teaching Archaeology in the 21st Century: Thoughts on Graduate Education," 17(1): 21-22; Phyllis E. Messenger et al., March 1999, "Teaching Archaeology in the 21st Century: Thoughts on Postgraduate Education/Professional Development," *SAA Bulletin* 17(2):13-14]

III.
FRAMING DISCUSSIONS:
Considering the Contexts

DISCIPLINARY CONTEXTS: THINKING ABOUT SOURCES AND DIRECTIONS FOR CHANGE

The premise of our curricular proposal is that changing contexts for the practice of archaeology in the late twentieth century require that we reexamine how and what we teach students of archaeology in undergraduate and graduate curricula. Moreover, we assert that these changes are profound enough to generate a need for a coherent program of professional development seminars dealing with related issues for practicing archaeologists. This thesis is not necessarily a comfortable one for an academic discipline whose practice has changed over the years mainly in response to intellectual currents within the discipline (see, for example, Willey and Sabloff 1993 or Trigger 1989). The purpose of this section is, then, to support our thesis by identifying those contexts that we believe have been responsible for altering the shape and direction of archaeological practice and articulating their impacts on the discipline and implications for its pedagogy. The contexts that the authors in this section treat include the ethical issues that all archaeologists must confront in their work, the missions of the organizations employing them, and the social and political concerns of the communities in which they are likely to conduct their work. Through such discussion, the authors are able to identify the demands and responsibilities that these various contexts place on those who teach archaeology to future professionals or the educated laypersons whose support of the discipline will be critical to its future well-being. The following section then provides commentary from several authors who have attempted to address these contexts in their academic curricula.

References Cited

Trigger, B. G.
   197   *A History of Archaeological Thought*. Cambridge University Press, Cambridge.

Wiley, G. R., and J. Sabloff
   1993   *A History of American Archaeology*. W.H. Freeman, New York.

Training students in Archaeological ethics

Mark J. Lynott and Vincas P. Steponaitis

Ethics are the rules or standards that govern the conduct of the members of a profession. Until recently, archaeological ethics have been oriented to a profession dominated by academia. Formal ethical training has been generally limited, and the training which has been offered has been aimed largely at concerns of the academic community. Archaeology has changed a great deal during the last 25 years. This is most obvious in the wide range of positions and jobs in which archaeologists are employed. As long as most archaeological activities were conducted within the sphere of university departments, students were trained in skills that were important to their future careers as university professors. Ethical training at these times was generally informal. As such students learned about ethics from peers, observing their academic mentors, and experimentation.

Passage of the National Historic Preservation Act in 1966 changed the environment for archaeology in the United States immensely. While this change was somewhat gradual over two decades, the dramatic nature of this change cannot be ignored. Archaeologists are now working in an increasingly wide range of jobs, and constantly facing new challenges to their professionalism and ethics. Many of the challenges facing archaeologists today are new and were not anticipated 25 years ago (e.g., repatriation, archaeology as business), and many of the challenges have been around for decades but have metamorphosed into larger and more complex problems (e.g., commercialization of the archaeological record). Even the most well-intentioned individuals are frequently faced with ethical challenges for which there is often no clear or well-understood precedent.

The need for ethical guidance among contemporary archaeological practitioners has been advocated by the Society of Professional Archaeologists since 1976. The Society for American Archaeology, recognizing that an updated ethics policy and a more active approach to ethics was needed, adopted eight Principles of Archaeological Ethics (Lynott 1997; Lynott and Wylie 2000).

Ethics and Gray Areas

Ethical policies may be addressed in two very different ways. The Society of Professional Archaeologists has developed their Code of Ethics and Standards of Research Performance. This is a very specific code that specifies desired conduct or behavior in terms of "an archaeologist shall," and specifies undesirable conduct as "an archaeologist shall not." This type of code specifies minimally acceptable standards of behavior or conduct, which Wylie (1996) describes as "floors." The SAA Principles of Archaeological Ethics represent "ceilings," or ethical ideals. It is understood that these goals or ideals may not be easily achieved in everyday archaeological practice, but they should be used to direct professional activities amid the complexities of our constantly changing world.

Because of the nature of ethical issues, it often is very difficult to codify and clearly define regulations to direct or curtail certain types of professional activities. Consequently, discussion and dialogue about ethical issues are important, and necessary to build a consensus among professional practitioners. Ethical policies that lack support from professional practitioners are likely to be ineffective. Consequently, the SAA Ethics Committee is responsible for encouraging discussion about ethical issues and bringing ethical concerns to the attention of the archaeological community.

Formal Training

The need for formal training on archaeological ethics cannot be overemphasized. Some university colleagues have argued that advancing the cause of archaeology will be accomplished by publishing more and better research. They are not persuaded by arguments that universities and archaeology will be advanced by the increased success of students who are able to take what they have learned and use it in a practical and professional way in the world outside academia. In the long term, universities will be judged not only by the publications of the faculty they employ, but also by the success of the students they graduate.

Any university that is concerned with the future success of their students is obliged to provide those students with training in archaeological ethics. Very few graduating archaeologists will find employment as researchers and teachers in universities and colleges. If they hope to use their skills in archaeology, most graduates will have to look for work in cultural resource management, either in the private sector or a government agency. They will be expected to regularly use skills they were never taught in school, and deal with issues and concerns which never affect an archaeologist in an academic position. If they are not properly prepared for the challenges of this large and diverse workplace, and are forced to rely upon skills and ethics which are narrowly adapted for university circumstances, there is a strong possibility that they will be unsuccessful. Unsuccessful employees reflect poorly on the institution from which they have graduated, and may limit or reduce the opportunities for employment of future graduates from that institution.

Yet the question remains: how and at what level should this ethical training be provided? At the undergraduate level, most archaeology in the United States is taught in liberal arts programs. The primary goal of such programs is to teach students how to think and write effectively; imparting skills geared to a specific profession is of secondary concern. Thus, while archaeological ethics is certainly a suitable subject for undergraduate coursework (e.g., it forms an excellent case study of how one weighs ethical principles in solving real-world problems), one could argue that it need not be a major focus of undergraduate archaeology programs. As a practical matter, every undergraduate who takes an archaeology course should probably hear the message against looting, and enough background to understand why that message is important. But consideration of other ethical issues that affect professional practice in archaeology can hardly be considered essential, particularly given that a bachelor's degree is generally not considered a professional credential in our field.

It is at the graduate level that students in the United States are trained to become professionals, and so it is at this level that formal training in ethics should be offered. The ideal is to make a broad consideration of ethical issues part of every graduate student's classroom experience. Yet this ideal is more the exception than the rule. In some cases, the main obstacle to implementing this ideal is inertia: faculty tend to teach in the manner that they themselves were taught, and ethics has not traditionally been taught in the classroom. In other cases, the obstacle is time: there is so much to teach, and so little time in which to do it. Students don't want to remain in graduate school forever, and often faculty are already stretched to the limit teaching the courses that are currently required. We maintain, however, that neither of these obstacles is insurmountable. It may be that only the larger graduate programs will have the faculty resources to offer routinely an entire course on archaeological ethics. But any credible graduate program, no matter how small, can add at least some consideration of archaeological ethics to the courses that they now require their students to take. Needless to say, this addition will require devoting less time to other subjects currently being taught. But given the importance of the issues involved, we believe that this shift in priorities is essential.

Practicing What We Preach

The need for more emphasis upon ethics in formal education also is illustrated by the limited instances where ethics have been taught in archaeological education programs. Most archaeological training has taught that we are obliged to develop a research design, excavate in a systematic manner, take good notes, and preserve the records and collections from our research for future study. However, in actual practice, archaeologists have all too often failed to live up to those standards. Brian Fagan (1995) has written about what he calls "archaeology's dirty little secret." Although everyone in archaeology knows it is important to prepare a report on our research, why are there so many reports which remain incomplete or never even started? Field schools have been notorious for this transgression, but nearly everyone has at least one report on their research that needs to be finished.

The collections and records which result from our research represent the only opportunity by which a colleague can examine our research and agree or disagree with our interpretations. Consequently, we have always taught that it is important to make good notes and records and ensure that collections are kept in good order for future study. However, in reality, archaeological collections are in poor condition throughout much of the United States. Anyone who has actually tried to restudy collections from previous research has probably been frustrated with the condition of the collections and the lack of supporting archival information. Since the records and collections from our research represent the mechanism by which our interpretations may be verified, it is critical to our claims that archaeology is a science that we maintain these materials in good order.

Most archaeological students have been at least introduced to the concept that we have a professional obligation to prepare a report on our research and ensure that the collections and records from our research are preserved for future study. Why then are these highly important ethical concepts treated so lightly in everyday practice? Could it be because archaeologists have learned about these concepts from observing the behavior of their own mentors, professors, and supervisors? Elevating ethics training to be a part of formal archaeological education might help to resolve this problem. After all, isn't one of the best ways to ensure that we understand a particular concept, is to try to explain it or teach it to someone else?

Conclusions

Despite our best intentions and efforts, it is impossible to generate an ethics code that will specify proper and improper behavior for all potential situations that archaeologists may face in our world today. Circumstances that affect archaeology are constantly changing, and we cannot ever fully anticipate the issues which might arise. With a few notable exceptions, archaeologists ignored Native American concerns about the study of human remains and cemeteries, and those concerns were eventually manifested in legislation that profoundly affects the nature and amount of archaeological research we can do. Hopefully, the passage of the Native American Graves Protection and Repatriation Act has taught us that we cannot assume that we control the archaeological record and its use, and that we must interact with the public and the special interest groups to ensure that the archaeological record is used and preserved in the best interests of all humankind.

Archaeology has changed a great deal in the last three decades. The diverse range of positions in which archaeologists are now employed make it impossible to closely specify appropriate professional behavior for all possible circumstances. SAA's Principles of Archaeological Ethics were developed to serve as a beacon in the turbulent and constantly changing circumstances archaeologists face today. However, since these principles are quite general in nature, and are not intended to be the final word on archaeological ethics, it is essential that archaeologists stay informed about ethical issues through an ongoing dialogue about ethics. Every archaeologist needs to enter the workplace with a basic understanding of current ethical issues in archaeology. This understanding can be best developed in formal academic training, where proper ethical conduct should receive just as much attention as method and theory. A growing number of books and papers about ethics and ethical issues are available (e.g. Messenger 1989; Vitelli 1996; Woodall 1990), and university curricula needs to be refined to incorporate these timely and important issues.

References Cited

Fagan, B.
1995   Archaeology's Dirty Little Secret. *Archaeology* 48(4): 14-17.

Lynott, M.J.
1997   Ethical Principles and Archaeological Practice: Development of an Ethics Policy. *American Antiquity* 62:589-599.

Lynott, M.J., and A. Wylie (editors)
2000   *Ethics in American Archaeology.* 2nd rev. ed. Society for American Archaeology, Washington, D.C.

Messenger, P.M.
1989   *The Ethics of Collecting Cultural Property. Whose Culture? Whose Property?* University of New Mexico Press, Albuquerque.

Vitelli, K.D. (editor)
1996   *Archaeological Ethics.* AltaMira Press, Walnut Creek.

Woodall, J. N.
1990   *Predicaments, Pragmatics and Professionalism: Ethical Conduct in Archaeology.* Special Publication No. 1. Society of Professional Archaeologists, Oklahoma City.

Wylie, A.
1996   Ethical Dilemmas in Archaeological Practice: Looting, Repatriation, Stewardship, and the (Trans)formation of Disciplinary Identity. *Perspectives on Science* 4(2):154-194.

Archaeological Education and Private Sector Employment

Joseph Schuldenrein and Jeffrey H. Altschul

There is no question but that the transition from academic archaeological training to the workplace is challenging and demanding for employer and employee alike. This axiom holds for any profession requiring advanced training. Freshly minted neophytes from lawyers, doctors, and engineers to journalists, filmmakers, and fashion designers, echo the same refrain: "They never told me it would be like this in the real world." Is it any different for archaeologists?

The unqualified answer would appear to be "yes." While the training path for each of the aforementioned professions combines strong academic focus with "in-field" empirical experiences over the course of a graduate/professional school career, archaeological programs largely do not. Long-term programs (i.e., those requiring 3 years or more of post-undergraduate schooling) such as medical school require residencies and internships while law school arranges or builds in "clerking." Shorter term programs such as journalism and film structure more compact programs and offer their students assignments to newspapers and studios. In short order, students are out on the street, testing the market on the strength of skills acquired in school, lessons learned in apprenticeship, and networks already initiated in the professional world.

For the most part, university archaeological programs offer none of these pathways. This is not to say that students do not pick up practical skills along the way; most do. However, they do this not because of the formal requirements of a department, but sometimes in spite of it. For survival reasons, students must pick up "job skills" that will require them to ease into the CRM world. Yet, they often do this at the expense of advancing in degree programs, at the risk of incurring the wrath of advisers and violating department protocol, and on their own time. The dilemma is especially grievous for long-term students (i.e., those in PhD programs) where structure is eliminated after attainment of ABD status and the march to the dissertation is a long, energy-consuming, and often obsessive ordeal that leaves little time for the pursuit of employment-related training.

Private Sector Employment:
Job Categories and Advancement

To assess the profound conflict between academic progress and advancement in the private sector, it is necessary to understand the structure of the CRM workplace and the skills required for functioning in that environment. Generally, CRM firms employ archaeology professionals in one of six essential job categories, hierarchically ranked as follows:

1) Field/lab technicians
2) Field/lab supervisors
3) Field/lab director
4) Principal investigator
5) Project manager
6) Firm principals/department heads

Field/lab technicians have a bachelor's-level education and tend to shuttle between projects and organizations. They are undergraduates who have recently earned their degree, junior graduate students, or belong to a growing group of itinerant laborers whose objectives are to hone field skills and practice "dirt archaeology." In the past, these were not considered career positions in and of themselves. Today, there is a growing number of people who have decided to remain at this level as a career choice. Field/lab supervisors, the next level, have developed substantial expertise and are responsible for groups of 4 to 5 people. They are typically semi-permanent to permanent employees of a going concern, also B.A. educated. Directors are responsible for the day-to-day operations of a project and coordinate efforts among field supervisors. They are invariably permanent employees of the firm and will typically have substantial writing responsibility; many have M.A.s but some do not. Principal investigators are senior members of CRM firms or of the CRM division in larger organizations. They must hold a M.A. degree; many have Ph.D.s. They assume professional and technical accountability for all projects in which they function in that capacity. They may be minimally involved in day-to-day operations, but must claim synthetic grasp of the project; they may or may not have business accountability. Project managers may not have advanced degrees but always have the ultimate responsibility for guiding projects from proposal inception to final write up. They are generally dedicated to business and administrative responsibilities and fiscal accountability. Finally, as owners, firm principals oversee all aspects of the CRM firm's operation. In larger companies, department heads perform the same tasks, although they may have more limited ownership in the company.

Ironically, while the aforementioned hierarchy is ordered by progressive financial remuneration, it does not necessarily reflect increasing archaeological expertise or even involvement. There is actually an inverse relationship between archaeological responsibility and compensation at the upper levels. Thus, project managers often will have less archaeological expertise than principal investigators, but they have more responsibility for the overall project; they generally earn more money and are accorded higher status. Firm principals may have started out as archaeological professionals but have evolved into business people exclusively. They may not have M.A. degrees and in some instances they are not even archaeologists or CRM professionals.

The underlying message here is that the archaeological trajectory in and of itself will typically peak at the principal investigator level. After that stage, it is business acumen and experience that account for a large measure of career advancement in the CRM arena. It should be noted, however, that many principal investigators, with excellent archaeological credentials, hold dual titles as project managers and principal investigators. Dual responsibilities are generally conferred after extensive service with a major CRM firm and only after the individual has learned the necessary business skills over a period of several years. Many older principal investigators cannot make the move because of deficits in their business knowledge. Graying principal investigators are frequently PhDs who have spent peak years completing doctorates and are disinclined to learning the skills necessary for making the leap.

CRM Employment and Academic Training: A Match Made on Mars?

Why, then, are our Ph.D. archaeologists not receiving the training they need to advance systematically in the working environments that will employ at least 70 to 80 percent of them in the next millennium (Zeder 1997)? One need not look any farther than the nearest Ph.D. program at a major university.

In most first-rate institutions, academic training programs are dynamic and reflect methodological and theoretical advances that have dominated the discipline. Such compelling developments as postprocessualism, gender archaeology, and ethnoarchaeology are making invaluable contributions to our conceptualizations of archaeology. There have been several volumes on the theme of "Rethinking Archaeology" in recent years.

In CRM, however, we need to do archaeology and do it efficiently. Of course, we need to think about it, but we need to do our cognitive work as we move along in the practice of survey, testing, and excavation. More significantly, the new engine driving archaeology is no longer the research institute or funding agency but state and federal coffers whose charge is dictated by preservation law and compliance. For the profession in general, research agendas are no longer selected by professors; they are imposed by planners.

However, the dominant academic paradigm is, as the popular cultural refrain hearkens, "stuck in the '60s." Elsewhere, a coauthor of this essay has underscored the bankruptcy of that paradigm, which was driven by an expanding, leisure-class economy that accommodated increasing academic jobs and encouraged exotic, albeit highly productive research

(Schuldenrein 1995). It is unclear whether or not most departments realize that their charges should have changed in the past 30 years. They still dedicate their efforts to training students to become researchers and teachers, despite a complete realignment in the archaeological workplace. It has been claimed, however myopically, that those faculty who run departments and were trained in the '60s and early '70s are simply unaware of the changing employment climate. Others argue that self-preservation and stagnation account for an inertia that prevents academicians from confronting the revamped archaeological workplace. Such assessments notwithstanding, the continued production of growing numbers of students to fill dwindling academic slots is misinformed at best and deceitful at worst. Yet it goes on.

The time-worn argument that a university's mission is to teach archaeologists to think and not to serve as vocational training grounds begs the issue sorely and bespeaks elitist arrogance, at a time when the cost, effort, and duration of Ph.D. training is greater than ever before and offerings for traditional jobs have never been as meager. Informal surveys of graduate programs show that the course types taught at most institutions do not differ qualitatively from those taught over the past 30 years. Introductory core courses are followed by "method and theory" offerings reflecting the specialty and regional interests of the professors who teach at a given institution.

Public Archaeology:
Who Are We Serving Anyway?

A corollary of the academic paradigm described above is a deeply held belief by many archaeologists that the primary mechanism for transmitting the results of their work is academically oriented journals and books. Making the results of archaeology accessible to the public is viewed as a secondary goal, if recognized at all. One might argue that CRM professionals might be more sensitive to this issue simply because their livelihoods are tied to public support of historic preservation. Public interest in archaeology, however, dates back to the founding of this country. Federal support for archaeological research also is of long standing, with funding for CRM-type project dating back to the Great Depression. Large-scale, academically inspired research projects, such as those funded by the National Science Foundation, actually are quite recent in origin. Even these projects are somewhat anomalous. As Rogge (1981) points out, during the heyday of NSF large projects in the 1960s (with the exception of one year), NSF expenditures for archaeological research were always smaller than the budget for internal projects (i.e., CRM-type projects) at the National Park Service.

While history suggests that the entire discipline should be concerned with public outreach, why should CRM firms be concerned with training in public archaeology? To a certain extent, the need is self-serving. We want to keep the public interested in archaeology and we need to have people on our staffs who know how to accomplish this goal. A second need comes in the form of contracts. Federal agencies are increasingly asking contractors for services in public outreach. These services can take the form of popular writing, volunteer archaeological programs, or classroom materials. Most CRM firms try to meet these needs with their staff, with, not surprisingly, mixed results. Academically trained archaeologists do not know much about curriculum development, teaching methods, or nontechnical writing. Often, it feels as if we are trying to push the square peg into the round hole. To better serve these needs, a greater emphasis should be made to cross-list courses between departments of anthropology, museum studies, and education.

Changing Course(s) for the Next Millennium

There appears to be no programmatic alternative to altering trends in contemporary training for graduate education in archaeology. By the same token, it is neither productive nor realistic to assume that the structure of the existing university system will be overhauled by the tugs of the marketplace. Clearly, the academic and private sector communities must make several compromises to ensure a successful transition, so that graduate education may better align with those sectors which show the most unequivocal signs of long-term expansion in this field. These would include the following steps.

Action items.

1) Initiate formal internship programs between universities and CRM companies. These would be required for degree programs and officially recognized by departments in the form of credits and satisfaction of formal requirements.

2) Revise course requirements for archaeologists in anthropology departments. These would include offerings in other fields such areas as preservation law, ethics, business, and proposal writing. It also would include mandatory revisions in archaeology curricula to include courses on statistics, sampling, and GIS, all skills that will be indispensable in the next few years.

3) Replace open faculty lines (through retirement or attrition) by accomplished CRM professionals. The latter would be capable of teaching CRM and more general courses. Critically, they should be able to offer career advancement guidance to graduate students.

4) Streamline and pare down Ph.D. programs. There are simply too many Ph.D.s out on the market.

5) Develop courses and programs in public education that will enable students to interact with local communities. Students should be encouraged to pursue careers that will bring them in touch with the public, the eventual source of most archaeological funding in the long term.

professional education and training for public service archaeology

Francis P. McManamon

Public agencies at all levels need professional archaeologists. The functions of such professional staff range from developing and overseeing public policy, to managing programs and resources, to carrying out archaeological investigations and conducting research. Effective performance in these kinds of positions requires individuals who:

- know archaeology theory, method, technique, and substance;
- are articulate and can write clear, concise English;
- translate clearly between the scientific jargon of archaeology and everyday English; and,
- know public laws and policies, regulations, and guidelines as they relate to anthropology, archaeology, curation, historic preservation, and related fields.

Formal professional training to create these kinds of knowledge, abilities, and expertise through existing graduate programs in anthropology and archaeology is the approach to take, rather than creating a separate professional, graduate program in cultural resource management (CRM) or "heritage management." Within the U.S. legal framework for protecting, preserving, interpreting, and commemorating archaeological resources, determinations of the importance of the resources requires judgments based upon information or commemorative value. The professional ability to make such judgments requires formal education and training in anthropology and archaeology. The successful completion of formal programs of study and the attainment of professional certificates or academic degrees provide the public recognition of such ability.

Existing graduate educational programs in anthropology and archaeology need to be modified to provide the needed kinds of expertise and experience. However, careful readers will note that of the four areas identified above, only historic preservation might be considered to focus specifically on the special knowledge and experience related directly to public archaeology.

Archaeologists who work for public agencies require the same kinds of professional knowledge and abilities to use archaeological theory, method, and techniques as archaeologists who work at colleges, museums, and consulting firms. This also is true for their knowledge of archaeological interpretations of a particular geographical region(s), time period(s), or special archaeological technique, such as dating, lithic analysis, and so on. Academic departments with graduate and professional education programs certainly all strive to provide these kinds of knowledge and experience to their students.

The ability to express oneself clearly and translate between the necessary professional jargon of archaeology and everyday English are useful skills for all archaeologists. These abilities are critically important for archaeologists working in public agencies because these professionals are called upon daily to interact effectively with nonarchaeologists. Frequently, public-sector archaeologists are required to explain archaeological method, techniques, or results to nonarchaeologists who will make decisions about the fate of archaeological resources. Often, public-sector archaeologists will be required to translate the results of archaeological investigations into everyday English for specialists in other fields—e.g., engineers, interpreters, law enforcement staff, and planners. Typically, public-sector archaeologists also must describe the results of agency archaeological investigations or the importance of the archaeological resources cared for by the agency in ways that enable the general public to understand, appreciate, and support the outcome public agencies' efforts. For those graduate students who aim for public-sector positions, professors must take special care that the learning of specialized terms, methods, and techniques does not replace existing abilities for common communication. For those students who lack the ability to communicate effectively, public-sector work may not be the correct avenue for them unless they can develop this skill.

Expertise in public laws, policies, and regulations and their implementation is an area of training that graduate programs need to develop or expand. Unlike many of my colleagues now in public-sector positions, I did have a two-semester, graduate-level seminar dealing with these public archaeology topics, at least as they existed in 1975. Graduate courses in public-sector topics are needed to provide professional knowledge in policies, laws, and regulations; the organization, administration, and functions of public agency programs; and the history of the development of public policy in archaeology and historic preservation. These are examples, not a comprehensive list of topics. Public-sector archaeologists with special expertise in these kinds of topics and ability to teach graduate-level courses can assist in developing and providing such courses.

In my own experience, I found that I really learned about the implementation of public archaeology in two ways. One, during my graduate training, I undertook all aspects of a small CRM project, under the tutelage of my graduate adviser, who was an expert in the topic. Second, after I had left campus, I worked as an archaeologist in the Massachusetts State Historic Preservation Office. Based upon these experiences, I note the usefulness, even necessity, of these kinds of educational experiences. Internships or work-study assignments in local, state, national, or international archaeology or CRM programs, and responsibility for small public archaeology projects—from planning through final report completion, under the direction of a faculty expert—can provide important insights and experience for training students in public-sector archaeology. Such "hands-on" experiences should be part of graduate education for archaeologists heading for the public sector. Academic departments should look to public-sector archaeologists for help in arranging for such work experiences.

On a more general level, we should remember that CRM incorporates public-sector archaeology, but also includes other kinds of cultural resources—e.g., historic structures, traditional places, public sculpture, and museum objects. Conceived broadly, CRM involves a range of disciplines, all of them also requiring certain distinct professional training and experiences. It seems unlikely that individual academic departments of anthropology or archaeology will want to expand to cover all of these kinds of expertise. However, a group of academic departments might work together to develop an interdisciplinary CRM program and thus cover the topic more broadly than any single department.

Public-sector archaeology graduate training also should allow for students to fill out their own educational programs through professional-level courses in other departments if there is not a broad CRM program available. I have found it very helpful in my own career to have background and a genuine interest in American history, historical architecture, and museum collections. This kind of knowledge, whether from a formal educational setting or through personal reading and interest, is helpful for substance, context, and the establishment of professional and personal relationships with colleagues in history, historical architecture, and museum management.

The Government Sector: Reforming the Archaeology Curriculum to Respond to New Contexts of Employment

James J. Miller

The government sector provides diverse and rapidly growing opportunities for professional archaeological employment. In recognition of the unique characteristics of government employment, we often call this practice cultural resource management (CRM) or public archaeology. These fields contrast fundamentally with the traditional model of archaeological education, which may be characterized, only somewhat facetiously, as the training of archaeology students by professors of archaeology to produce more professors of archaeology to train more students. Real progress has already been made in revising some academic programs to include cultural resource management topics, and many university students obtain experience in cultural resource projects during their education, sometimes outside the curriculum. Yet there is a wide difference between the knowledge, skills, and abilities necessary to function effectively as a cultural resource manager in the government sector, and the preparation of students in most graduate programs in anthropology/archaeology.

If we represent the archaeology and cultural resource management fields as a Venn diagram, there is an area of overlap, and there are areas that are exclusive to each of the fields. The overlap represents those aspects of professional practice that are necessary for both: it would be highly unlikely in these modern times to obtain a graduate degree without some exposure to and understanding of cultural resource management activities, at least at a local level; and the converse is even more unlikely—there can be no cultural resource management without a thorough grounding in archaeology. An effective curriculum must identify and incorporate those basic elements of both fields which constitute a minimum level of training to serve in either field. In contrast, there are aspects of training and employment for one field which are not necessary or appropriate for the other. These represent the ways in which the fields are justifiably different—skills necessary for successful academic employment are not the same as those required for cultural resource management. Strategies of professional advancement are very different in the university and in the bureaucracy. Interpersonal relationships are different, opportunities and obligations to interact with the public are different, responses to political considerations are different, and so on. To the extent that we expect students to function in a government employment context who are familiar only with an academic employment context, we are failing the students, the public, and eventually the sites.

What, then, are the necessary components of a curriculum that would prepare students to serve as effective cultural resource managers; which of these should be mastered by all archaeology students, and which are unique to cultural resource management? There are a few university programs that have been training students specifically in cultural resource management for many years, and students who decide early in their university careers to pursue a CRM track have some choices in their selection of graduate departments. However, these account for a small proportion of the people around the country who become cultural resource managers in the government sector. Many of the people who are successful government job applicants could be better prepared for their new responsibilities. There are a number of skills which are not recognized as important in graduate school that are crucial in government employment.

1) *All students with an advanced degree should have a basic command of the archaeological cultures in the state or region for which they would be responsible, including their temporal and spatial organization, environmental history, and artifact characteristics.* It is surprising how seldom this is true.

2) *All students should recognize that cultural resource management is not second-rate archaeology.* It is a serious profession in its own right, deserving the full commitment and dedication of the employee for an honorable and respectable purpose.

3) *A well-prepared student will understand the fundamental difference between working in an academic context and working in a government context.* Neither is necessarily better than the other: they are simply very different, and the skills that work in one will not likely work so well in the other.

4) *Students must come prepared with the intellectual and analytical tools required for the job.* It surprises many archaeologists to learn that they are poor writers, and that their academic styles of expression are ineffective outside the university. In fact, upon close examination, it often turns out that jargon and complex constructions are simply devices to conceal sloppy thinking. It is essential that all archaeology students know how to understand the nature of information, formulate a relevant question, select and analyze the necessary facts, arrive at a logical conclusion, and express it in a clear, concise manner for the person who is unfamiliar with the subject area. What's more, these skills must produce their product in a matter of minutes or hours, not often

weeks or months. All students should realize that archaeology is not a fundamental truth, or even a common way of approaching reality. It is a peculiar perspective that can be brought to bear on a narrow subset of human situations.

In cultural resource management, the purpose of applying the tools of our craft is much more often site conservation and public education than increase and diffusion of knowledge. The effective cultural resource manager will need to know how to interact with people from many other disciplines in the government and private sectors as well as with the public in all its wonderful diversity. A well-prepared student will understand the principles of public service and their role in decision making. A basic appreciation of the legal framework of cultural resource management is essential, as is an appreciation that decisions in the public sector are limited and compelled by laws which represent public consensus rather than archaeological opinion.

Strategies for revising the archaeology curriculum to respond to new contexts of government employment must fit within the academy. Archaeologists will not change the structure of universities but can find many opportunities to adapt existing institutions to accomplish their goals.

1) *Cultural resource management curricula should remain within archaeology programs.* A thorough understanding of archaeological method, theory, and regional content is essential.

2) *The curricula should recognize the much broader scope of cultural resource management and should incorporate experts from other fields such as business, ecology, law, and public administration.* These specialists should adapt their expertise to the cultural resource management curriculum rather than relying on the student to take a course intended to train one for a different discipline. For example, faculty from the law school, the public administration department, and the business school might team teach a course on historic preservation and cultural resource management law to explain the legal and economic realities of professional practice.

3) *Non-university people should be brought into the program so that students gain a better understanding of the operations of government and business.* Cultural resource managers from federal, state, and local government agencies and the private sector should be available not only to lecture, but also to involve students in projects or internships and advise on employment opportunities.

4) *In some cases, it will be appropriate to extend the program beyond the department to form an institute or graduate group that can provide advanced or specialized instruction on a larger scale.* Topics like archaeological law enforcement, grant writing

and administration, large project management, public land management, public interpretation, and so on can be offered within traditional coursework, but also as professional development courses for professionals in many fields who are no longer full-time students.

5) *Once such an institute is established, it should provide education and training for people who manage cultural resources but who are not cultural resource managers.* In reality, the decisions and actions that directly affect archaeological sites are most often made by agency administrators, foresters, law enforcement officers, park managers, and others whose understanding of archaeology reflects general public knowledge rather than a professional perspective. In terms of site protection, the return on investment for such training is great and is an essential component of any effective educational model for cultural resource management.

community Relations: what the practicing Archaeologist needs to know to work effectively with local and/or descendant communities

Joe Watkins, K. Anne Pyburn, and Pam Cressey

rchaeology's quest to teach understanding of the past must be more than solely an academic exercise. Involvement of local and descendant communities is something archaeologists must learn to cultivate. Throughout the following position paper, we discuss what we feel future practitioners of all branches of archaeology—not just public archaeology, cultural resource management, or archaeology in the public interest—must be able to do: understand the communities with which they work, develop synergistic relationships with such communities, explain their programs in such a way that communities will support rather than isolate them.

Public archaeology, cultural resource management, archaeology in the public interest—whatever one wishes to call it—truly no longer operates within an insulated federal capsule separated from pure research archaeology. In fact, we can no longer sustain any distinction between these "archaeologies" and any kind of professional and ethical archaeology. Local communities now wield considerable influence in situations that were once totally under the control of the archaeologist, and public opinion often emerges against so-called "pure" scientific reasons for cultural resource management decisions. The public furor over Kennewick Man is an excellent example.

Overview of the Issues

There are several related professional reasons why archaeologists need involvement with local communities. The most obvious include the need to encourage preservation, develop an educated constituency, and attract the next generation of scholars to the discipline from a wider pool. What must future practitioners of archaeology learn?

1) *First and foremost—-respect*. Respect for views other than their own. Respect for cultures about which they might not be fully schooled. Respect for others' rights and beliefs. And respect for traditions which might conflict with their own.

2) *An intensive course in ethics is of tantamount importance as a*

part of any archaeological program. Ethics in archaeology, ethics in anthropology, fieldwork ethics, ethics in bioanthropology, ethics in public archaeology—take your pick—but practitioners *must* be exposed to situations which force them to question assumed and unexamined notions concerning what they do and how they do it. They must be prepared to answer gracefully and confidently questions and criticisms from interested groups. Unfortunately, students usually graduate and enter professional employment without ever examining issues related to the impact of their career path on people outside of their own systems of thought, let alone those within.

3) *Practitioners must be aware of the need to understand the various relationships among various portions of the community in which they will be working*. Archaeologists have power, based on the fact that their decisions about the treatment of issues of cultural heritage often prevail over those of untrained populations (Swidler et al. 1997). Local and descendant community members, on the other hand, often feel powerless to control much of what goes on around them. Either as a result of political or economic situations, descendant communities generally have little control over programs undertaken by archaeologists. Even when descendant communities might have political control, they generally rely on people with the proper "credentials" for informed opinions on which to base their decisions. While these relationships cannot be understood in large measure without firsthand knowledge of the power structures involved in the relevant communities, research and ethnographic study of them will allow archaeologists at least to understand the structures from which the problems have grown. Strong research methodology in applied anthropology, social anthropology, and ethnographic or sociological methods should, therefore, go hand-in-hand with any professional degree program in archaeology (Downum 1999; Pyburn and Wilk 1995).

4) *A strong sense of professionalism also must be developed*. Courses aimed at developing professionalism in archaeology can and should be extended from how to appear professional in presentations (paper presentation, visual aids, research methods, grant writing, and so forth) to include professionalism in the treatment of fellow archaeologists; professionalism in dealing with others less involved with the discipline; professionalism in handling the press; professionalism in presenting the research to local communities without patronizing nonspecialist audiences; and, finally, professionalism in ensuring the public is well served.

Students must learn how to reach out to local and descendant communities to develop lasting relationships. A key element missing from most archaeological research programs is a commitment of time: time to learn local values, history, and mores; and time to earn and establish trust. There are no "tricks" or shortcuts which can supplant honest communication and personal involvement with communities. While community size will determine the formality of the relationships, relationships must be developed nonetheless which will allow the smooth interaction of all parties involved.

Research should not be a one-way street, where the archaeologist determines the direction, speed, and destination of the project, but should be an integrated program that takes into consideration the varied viewpoints of those who have an interest in the research. A community-based research program, one which involves the community in as many stages of decision making as possible, will not only produce relevant research, but also will produce research which benefits the entire public. This also is the only sure route to long-term preservation of archaeological resources.

Rather than attempt to structure a generic program which would teach future practicing archaeologists how to deal with communities, we recommend that educational programs be developed that allow students to integrate adequately the community into their research—either via internships or through the conduct of an independent or collaborative research project. We feel that the practicing archaeologist should be able to identify the community with which they will be involved.

Action Item. **Identify the Community.**

Practicing archaeologists need the ability to develop an "ethnography of the community" as a participant and observer in a twenty-first century sense, so as to understand the bureaucratic and social processes that are involved in attaining the goal of their project. They must understand not only the governmental positions involved in the decision-making process on the community level (historic preservation officers, NAGPRA officers, planners, recreation specialists, transportation officers), but also the social and political pressures on the individuals who occupy those positions.

None of the goals of archaeological research can be met in the same way in all contexts. To ignore local values and mores is to take a colonialist attitude toward "subject" populations. For example, respect for local populations is clearly an important portion of any project and fundamental to research design and training students; but there is no simple formula for respectful behavior that will work in all cultural situations. It is crucial that projects include an ethnographic component that identifies appropriate behavior *before* attempts are made to "save the past" or educate the locals, and *before* inexperienced students are introduced into a local community, and that some means of sanctioning of staff, crew, and student behavior is available.

The importance of ethnographic knowledge cannot be stressed enough. Many professional archaeologists seem to have trouble understanding the difference between good intentions and respectful treatment of the public. For example, Armando Anaya's account (1998) of an incident in Chiapas in which local people attacked a group of archaeologists makes clear that the archaeologists were trying to do the "right" thing and intended a respectful attitude toward local people. However, they did not spend enough time gathering ethnographic data to realize that their actions were likely to provoke aggression. Instead, they focused on how to achieve a goal that they had set independently and for which they had secured limited support, i.e., from those people most likely to benefit. The use of ethnographic research to understand the morals, needs, and politics of a local area is expensive, time consuming, and may not always work. But like the scientific method, which also is expensive, time consuming, and does not always work, it is the best approach we have. All too often, good intentions pave the road to site destruction.

Action Item. Form Partnerships Beyond Archaeology.

It is important that the practicing archaeologist integrate the goals of the archaeological program with other community programs. It also is important that some goals developed by the researcher emanate from the community to provide the widest benefit to the most people. This process needs to involve not only underrepresented groups but also majority groups. In addition, the priorities of the project must be developed with the archaeologist acting as a representative of shared disciplinary goals. The SAA Committee on Ethics has placed stewardship at the top of the list of professional responsibilities. Stewardship may involve research, teaching, preservation, or repatriation, but protection of the archaeological record is the agreed-upon primary goal. Because funding for archaeological research is scarce, the impact of any single project will be great. There can be little quibbling about the ultimate commitment of any project.

Action Item. Understand the Legal Boundaries Involved in the Process.

The practicing archaeologist must know not only federal guidelines relating to cultural resource management, but also the local and/or descendant community processes that may affect the research project. Local planning and zoning ordinances, tribal codes, political history, and even social structures must be understood before a program can be integrated adequately into the community. While a great deal of this information can be learned prior to fieldwork, there are intangibles that can only be gathered after personal contact has been initiated.

Action Item. **Communicate Effectively.**

Communication to the widest range of audiences is the key to effective community integration. Presentations to professional colleagues are important to maintain academic involvement, but more important to community involvement is the ability to communicate effectively with any and all local groups. This requires oral presentations to a variety of audiences; publications written in the vernacular of the public, with easily understood terms and appropriate visual aides; displays and exhibits in public areas; and effective utilization of media outlets. Nor is an apparent lack of interest an excuse for ignoring local residents; under such circumstances, the archaeologist should consider ways of stimulating local interest, since this disinterest is likely to be a temporary situation that can quickly sour.

Action Item.
Recognize Diverse Decision-Making Structures.

We do not intend to discuss the issue of working with descendant communities separately, but it is necessary that archaeologists realize that local decisions in smaller communities often are made through a mixture of the common Western governmental system and more traditional systems. In some areas of the world, local church leaders will play an important role in community decisions, while in other areas traditional leaders will function as community leaders. It is important that the archaeologist be aware that not only elected and appointed individuals can sway public opinion, but that other social institutions function as de facto decision-making bodies.

For example, Watkins, in his role as an agency archaeologist for the Bureau of Indian Affairs of the federal government, must maintain relationships not only with the elected and appointed officials of several tribal governments, but also with leaders who maintain tribal traditions and generational knowledge. Consultation with traditional leaders is required by certain legislation, while a formal "government-to-government relationship" must be maintained in regard to other programs. It also is necessary that both sets of "governing bodies" be involved in consultation and program development so that neither set of specialized knowledge is ignored (Watkins and Parry 1997).

Action Item.
Place the Goals of the Project Ahead of Personal and Private Goals.

Often the project director has used a position of privilege (university association, government affiliation) to gain access to the archaeological record and introduce outsiders (the archaeological project members) into a local community, with the justification that the archaeological record is being preserved or probed. Allowing project members to behave in a way that discredits the project in the eyes of local people has negative repercussions for the future of the discipline and undermines the professional goals claimed for the issue of permits and grants. The presence of "outsiders" in a local community often has profound political, social, and psychological implications. In short, students must realize that their political statements in their behavior and dress on the campus of a U.S. university (e.g., about the equality of women or the evils of commercialism) may interfere with the goals of the archaeological project in some areas.

For example, Pyburn once shared an archaeological field station in a developing nation with a second archaeologist who was doing related work in the area. All visitors were required to renew their passports each month at the local police station. The second archaeologist was continuously irritated by the sexist treatment she received from local officials, who made inappropriate comments to her and invariably made her make two or three trips to town to get her passport stamped. This woman felt it was her right to dress in a manner that local residents saw as inappropriate to her gender and sexually provocative. Pyburn wore a modest dress and carried a "motherly" purse and got all the passports for her crew of 6 stamped at the same police station in about 10 minutes. Eventually she included the passport of her "liberated" colleague in the stack.

There is no question that the treatment of Pyburn and her colleague by the local police was sexist and politically disgusting, but Pyburn made a conscious decision to put the goals of the archaeological project above her political feelings about personal freedom. In her own projects, she recommends that students negotiate their own views of the local context outside the protection of the archaeological project if they wish to make political statements with their dress and behavior. Excavation, survey, photography, reconstruction—-these behaviors that are essential to archaeology are politically fraught enough that no extraneous issues need be included.

Gender issues often are highly charged within small societies and behavioral boundaries must be analyzed and handled with care. Although U.S. students might think of themselves as economically marginal and politically powerless, to people in many parts of the world, Americans are linked to power, freedom, and opportunity—-significant aphrodisiacs. American students might never realize that their attraction for local men can go far beyond simple sexuality. Local men or women may no longer be able to work on a project, because of the availability of "loose women," or disrespectful men, and archaeology can become associated in the minds of local residents with loose morals and exploitative behavior.

Female project directors may find it more difficult to gain respect and authority in the local area. Ultimately, a local movement to discourage archaeological research in the area can begin from such circumstances; there are even cases of site destruction perpetrated by local residents trying to keep archaeologists away.

Most practicing archaeologists will encounter only a few of these situations in the course of their careers, but it is necessary that all archaeologists be aware of the impact of their presence on a community. To work with and more effectively involve local and/or descendant communities, practicing archaeologists must examine their own preconceived notions concerning all these issues. Well-rounded education in all these areas will benefit not only archaeologists but also the communities they study by ensuring that all are involved in a program that is rooted in the values of the community in which it is seated.

The point also must be made that if archaeologists are going to accept public relations, educational outreach, and ethical research as central to their professional responsibilities, then a proactive stance on sex and gender is necessary. The ethical goals of public archaeology make archaeologists socially responsible for the messages they take into the present from the past. Caring for the archaeological record by establishing positive relations with local communities does not absolve archaeologists from their responsibility to teach with both their actions and their words. Emphasis on culturally appropriate behavioral guidelines for field projects must begin with training that makes archaeologists cognizant of their own cultural biases. The political repercussions of the unconscious validation of sexism among our publics and our students are detrimental to our discipline and to our world.

Archaeological data are some of our most powerful tools for influencing the reformulation of social, cultural, and gender stereotypes. Present-day essentialist constructions of social and gender groups frequently rely on assumptions and prejudices about the past, both historic and prehistoric, to justify differential treatment in the present. Current research on the origin and range of variation over time in differential treatment of individuals by status and role belie most essentialist constructions and open the door to new and healthier social formations. The fact is that archaeology as a discipline continues to foster the differential and unequal treatment of these social groups, either through the underrepresentation of women, first peoples, and people of color within its ranks, or by reifying political boundaries between genders and ethnic groups. However inadvertently, archaeologists participate in these issues, lack of understanding of their role is intolerable.

Numerous studies are available on male bias in the classroom, both in terms of course content and the treatment of students. Conkey and Gero (1997) have recently remarked on similar bias observed in an archaeological field school. Local communities that may provide the next generation of archaeologists, and our students, who are themselves a special kind of local community, deserve field directors and teachers who are sensitive to both local mores about gender and the repercussions of gender stereotyping as a means of interpreting the past or shaping the future.

Despite steps taken to address issues of diversity by both universities and federal agencies, the situation of economic, racial, and gender minorities in the discipline of archaeology continues to be unequal (Zeder 1997). What this means is that in addition to the implicit differences in the reward structure, there continue to be differences in our preparation of "white" and "non-white" and male and female students for professional life.

While few minority students enter university archaeology programs in large numbers (Franklin 1998), thus limiting the ethnic and racial diversity that public archaeology needs to enhance its vision (Ehrenhard 1998), even fewer minority students complete their degree programs and enter the profession. But even this lower number cannot be taken to explain the disparity in representation. Although female students enter university archaeology programs in comparable numbers, they achieve success as professionals at a much lower rate than men. This situation has more profound implications than employment opportunities for women within a small underfunded discipline; they reach far beyond and into the discipline's representation of itself and the past to the many publics that host its fieldwork and consume the knowledge that it generates.

Summary and Conclusions

We have argued that archaeological research is fundamentally a social undertaking. It involves both the field crew's social structure and project members' interactions with host community structure. Moreover, choices informing the composition of field crews and the character of their interactions with local communities may profoundly influence the knowledge produced by the project. From this perspective, the project director bears major responsibility for creating a climate in which fieldwork can proceed effectively and self-consciously. How do we train our students either to assume this critical disciplinary role or simply to become responsible members of a field crew? The answer would have to be unevenly, at best. We thus propose here several concrete curricular initiatives for revising student preparation for the field. They include course work that contains training in archaeological ethics and professionalism, as well as ethnographic field methods. Clearly it behooves all of us to consider these recommendations in the context of our own educational settings, since it is hard to deny the proposition that the social context in which archaeological research unfolds influences directly both the quality and efficiency of fieldwork and the validity of the knowledge that it generates.

References Cited

Anaya, A.
1998 Ethical and Moral Hazards of Doing Archaeology in Chiapas. *Anthropology Newsletter* 39(1):28-29.

Conkey, M. W., and J. M. Gero
1997 Programme to Practice: Gender and Feminism in Archaeology. *Annual Review of Anthropology* 26:411-437.

Downum, C. E., and L. J. Price
1999 Applied Archaeology. *Human Organization* 58(3):226-239.

Ehrenhard, J.
1998 Would Greater Ethnic and Racial Diversity Enhance Public Archaeology and Cultural Resource Management? Paper presented at the SAA Workshop on Teaching Archaeology in the Twenty-First Century, Wakulla Springs, Florida.

Franklin, M.
1998 Why Are There So Few Black American Archaeologists? Paper presented at the SAA Workshop on Teaching Archaeology in the Twenty-First Century, Wakulla Springs, Florida.

Pyburn, K. A., and R. R. Wilk
1995 Responsible Archaeology is Applied Anthropology. In *Ethics in American Archaeology: Challenges for the 1990s*, edited by M. J. Lynott and A. Wylie, pp. 71-76. Special Report. Society for American Archaeology, Washington, D.C.

Swidler, N., K. Dongoske, R. Anyon, and A. Downer (editors)
1997 *Native Americans and Archaeologists: Stepping Stones to Common Ground*. AltaMira Press, Walnut Creek.

Watkins, J., and T. Parry
1997 Archeology's First Steps in Moccasins. *Common Ground* 2(3/4): 46-49, Archaeology and Ethnology Program, National Park Service, Washington, D.C.

Zeder, M.
1997 *The American Archaeologist: A Profile*. AltaMira Press, Walnut Creek.

Archaeopolitics: The Political Context of Archaeology

Judith A. Bense

Why are politics important to archaeology? The short answer is because archaeology is almost totally dependent on politics, whether we like it or not. The overwhelming majority of the archaeology in the United States is done by, because of, or paid for by some part of the government which consists of people elected to office ("politicians"), the people they appoint to office, and their staffs. One of the primary goals of politicians is to get reelected. This means doing what it takes to get money and votes. Money and votes are essential to politicians.

Politics have been involved in archaeology since 1882 when the constituents of an Ohio member of Congress requested a bill for an archaeological study to determine the origin of the earth mounds in the eastern United States. The bill introduced by the congressman was passed, and $5,000 was appropriated to the newly formed Smithsonian Institution for a Mound Exploration Survey. The director of the Bureau of Ethnology, John Wesley Morgan, busy with ethnography in the Southwest, did not want to do the archaeology project. However, since the Bureau and the Smithsonian Institution of which it was a part was federally funded, he had no choice. To direct the survey, he hired Cyrus Thomas who did an excellent objective study that has stood the test of time. Since then, the union of archaeology and politics has only grown stronger (see Willey and Sabloff 1993 for further details).

Key federal legislation and regulations that have strengthened archaeology's political ties include the 1906 Antiquities Act, the federal archaeology program developed during the Depression, the 1966 National Historic Preservation Act, and the 1972 Archaeological Recovery Act (Moss-Bennet) Act. These last two acts placed archaeology among the responsibilities of every state historic preservation office and they funded compliance archaeology. They created the profession known as cultural resource management. While the amount of money spent on archaeology with public and private funds due to these federal laws and their regulations is not specifically calculated, they supply the funds for most federal archaeologists' salaries and pay for most of the archaeology projects done in this country. The long arm of the federal government reaches to the state and local level as well, requiring the funding and conduct of almost all state and local archaeology projects. In other words, politics in Washington pays the bills, and as a consequence, politicians control the funding of archaeological research in this country.

In higher education, the overwhelming majority of colleges, universities, and community colleges where archaeology is taught are funded by state governments. In addition, the large majority of research grants obtained by archaeologists who work in academic settings are state and federal program grants. As a result of this funding structure, state politicians pay the salary of almost all the teaching and research archaeologists in the country, and both state and congressional politicians pay for their research (cf. Zeder 1997:191-200). In other words, politicians are in the driver's seat in academics.

Evaluating the traditional undergraduate and graduate archaeology curriculum and the role that politics has played in it throughout the late twentieth century is easy. As paradoxical as it may seem, politics and its influence on archaeology has played only a very minor role, at best, in traditional archaeology education. Given the fact that archaeology in this country is *dependent* on *politics*, how could it NOT be part of our student training? That is the real question. One would think that mid-level and senior archaeologists who teach in institutions of higher education and know the structure of archaeological funding in the United States would want to pass their understanding on to their graduate students at the very least. If we do not train our students to be effective activists or advocates for archaeology in the political arena, then the politicians who ultimately control disciplinary funding will be free to direct such funds toward their own needs: distributing money to secure votes. The issue is not whether or not to include politics in archaeology, but how to educate and motivate students in this arena.

Should training in the political context of archaeology be "on the job" or imbedded in the curriculum? The answer is both. In fact, the first method is firmly in place. It is the only method by which students and new graduates consistently learn how politics affect archaeology. The majority of our graduates work in cultural resource management (CRM), either in the implementation (government) or compliance (consultant) area (Zeder 1997:47). They quickly experience, whether as a crew member, intern, field director, or site file assistant, how politics affects what they do in their job and how they do it. This on-the-job experience in politics should and will continue.

The academic curriculum in most universities and colleges has not significantly changed in this respect for three decades. In most departments, even a course in CRM is not taught. The reasons for this state of affairs appear to include the following:

1) Academic programs apply the four- (or three-) field approach to anthropological archaeology which, with advanced archaeology

courses, takes up the limited graduate course program.

2) Academic archaeologists generally do not take the time to understand the relationship between politics and archaeology as there is little incentive (publications for promotion, tenure, and raises) to spend the time and energy on getting involved. Therefore, these concerns are largely unknown to them and perceived as peripheral to the central focus of an academic training.

Personally, I am a politically active archaeologist at the local, state, and federal level where I previously served as chair of the SAA Government Affairs Committee. I understand how politics works and why it is important to archaeology. I embed the political context of archaeology in almost all archaeology courses, and specifically teach it in graduate courses (master's level), especially in CRM and Method and Theory. I also invite guest lecturers to contribute to the discussion in and out of class; usually these are individuals directly involved in the politics of archaeology such as Donald F. Craib, manager, Government Affairs and Counsel, for the Society for American Archaeology. I also require students to attend local city and county government public meetings that involve archaeology, such as the current debate over the use of metal detecting on city property. I give students Internet assignments on controversial topics such as the proposed amendment to NAGPRA to have them experience the effect of current political issues on archaeology.

Nonetheless, my approach is not common to college and university faculty, as noted above. The central issue seems to be convince these colleagues of the importance of understanding political contexts for the practice of archaeology among future professionals and then to provide them with interesting models for teaching about the various ways that archaeology and politics interact in the United States and abroad. I have listed a few ideas below which may suggest some low-cost tactics for introducing this subject into academic programs. They are a start at overcoming the inertia in academic curricula and stimulating the interest of research faculty.

1) *Revise or develop a course in Cultural Resource Management that both embeds the politics-archaeology union and has a section on governmental decision-making structures that affect archaeology.* Include a selection of the guest speakers listed below. Assign reading in *SAA Bulletin's* "Archaeopolitics" column.

2) *Develop a guest speaking program on Politics and Archaeology for archaeology students:*
state or local historic preservation officers (civics and archaeology) university lobbyist or the president (how things really get done)

scholar funded through national grant program (politics of grants)

CRM owners or managers (politics of implementation)

agency archaeologists (politics of implementation)

local grass roots political activist (making a political change)

panel of elected local, state, congressional officials (making an issue a priority)

panel of staffers of elected officials (how political change really happens)

3) *Develop a package of teaching materials for graduate and senior undergraduate classes on politics and archaeology within SAA— perhaps through the Government Affairs program—with video- tapes, handouts, and assignments for use in CRM or Method and Theory classes.* These products would explain the relationship of politics and archaeology and how the political system can be use to enhance the future of archaeology.

4) *Develop a publication on Archaeology and Politics* through SAA by a politically active archaeologist or lobbyist that is a unified entity (not selected papers), affordable, and kept up to date (3-year revisions).

5) *Sponsor Politics and Archaeology forums at state, regional, and national meetings.*

These few suggestions are just a beginning. Students must be prepared to deal effectively with the national, state, and local political systems that drive archaeology. And it is the responsibility of those of us who understand the potential of the archaeological record to ensure that teaching materials that introduce and explain the effects of politics on archaeology are readily available and relevant to the needs of colleagues teaching in a range of educational institutions throughout the United States.

References Cited

Willey, G. R., and J. A. Sabloff
1993 *A History of American Archaeology.* 3rd ed. W. H. Freeman, New York.
Zeder, M.
1997 *The American Archaeologist: A Profile.* AltaMira Press, Walnut Creek.

IV.
Archaeology Education into the Twenty-first Century:
Models for Change

overview of the issues

Kathleen M. Byrd and Ricardo J. Elia

The group of authors in this section was charged with the task of describing how we are attempting to incorporate public archaeology and cultural resource management (CRM) training into the academic programs at our institutions. Each of us has worked to create a program that provides students with the training requisite to becoming a CRM professional, either by enhancing existing academic curricula or by developing entirely new programs. Despite the variety of our approaches, they share one feature almost unique among graduate programs, a commitment to educating young professionals in the full range of activities included in archaeological practice in the early twenty-first century.

In archaeology education today, CRM and public archaeology—if they are taught at all—are introduced in a variety of ways. Many academic departments offer courses in CRM or public archaeology. Others offer internships or other employment and training opportunities through affiliated CRM organizations. Nonetheless, despite the burgeoning of CRM and public archaeology, relatively few academic departments offer specialized degree programs or other formal concentrations in this field. More than 30 years after the passage of the National Historic Preservation Act in the United States, only a handful of academic departments offer specialized degree training to prepare archaeological professionals for careers in public archaeology. The 1997-98 *Guide* of the American Anthropological Association lists, out of a total of 430 academic departments (mostly in the United States and Canada), four specialized master's programs in CRM or public archaeology; another two departments identify a CRM emphasis at the master's or graduate level (American Anthropological Association 1997). Four departments list undergraduate certificate programs in CRM, and another five have undergraduate concentrations or specialization in CRM or public archaeology.

In her profile of the American archaeology profession, based on a large survey sponsored by the Society for American Archaeology in 1994, Melinda Zeder (1997:208) identified "what is perhaps the core defining issue in American archaeology today—the apparently deepening division between archaeology practiced in academia and museums and that of archaeologists in the private and public sectors." A significant part of this division, according to Zeder, pertains to the education received by those who are now working in CRM and public archaeology:

> Nowhere was this disjunction more keenly expressed than
> in private and public sector levels of dissatisfaction with the
> adequacy of archaeologists' academic training as a prepara-

tion for their current careers, as well as in the tendency among these individuals to feel that their current careers do not match the original career expectations they held when entering the profession. Clearly, many of these people are convinced that the traditional academic training in archaeology is seriously out of step with the realities of archaeological practice today. Profiling student preferences and research interests gives special credence to the contention that academics are training future archaeologists primarily for careers in academia (Zeder 1997:208).

Each of us has attempted to develop formal academic programs in CRM and public archaeology at the master's level. Our approaches reflect the diversity of our four programs—two in departments of anthropology, one in history, and one in archaeology—and the various obstacles we faced in our particular academic institutions. Taken together, they probably cover most situations in academic departments that offer undergraduate and graduate degrees in archaeology.

In one program—probably typical of many, if not most, departments—an anthropology department offers a CRM course taught by adjunct faculty from an affiliated contract archaeology unit. The department's students benefit from employment and training opportunities with the contract unit, and the department receives revenue from the unit, but the unit remains funded on "soft money" and the department has been ambivalent about supporting a master's track in CRM archaeology.

A second academic program—this one in a history department—currently offers a CRM course to both undergraduate and graduate students, and is currently developing a new master's program in heritage resources. Two other departments currently offer specialized master's programs. One, an anthropology department focusing on applied anthropology, offers a master's in public archaeology, and is hoping to add a Ph.D. program. The other is a new master's in archaeological heritage management, offered in an archaeology, not anthropology, department.

Current Approaches

Below we briefly describe our current efforts to incorporate CRM and public archaeology education into our programs. More details about each program can be found in the individual papers.

The Anthropology Department of the College of William and Mary has made no formal, programmatic commitment to incorporate public archaeology or CRM as a specialized track in its curriculum. It did, however, introduce a course in CRM archaeology over 10 years ago and has modified existing courses with additional lectures or readings relating to CRM. The CRM course is team-taught by archaeologists from the William and Mary Center for Archaeological Research, an affiliated, self-supporting contract archaeology unit that offers employment and training opportunities for archaeology students.

Northwestern State University of Louisiana offers a course in CRM to both graduate and undergraduate students. This course deals with legislation and discusses tools that can be used to preserve both the archaeological and the built environment (e.g., conservation easements). The Master's Program in History with a CRM option requires a 2-semester, 20-hour-per-week internship with a federal, state, or local agency. Both undergraduate and graduate students are encouraged to participate in contract and grant projects. NSU is currently developing a new Master's Program in Heritage Resources; this program will be multidisciplinary and will include courses in history and the built environment, as well as archaeology and anthropology.

The Anthropology Department of the University of South Florida shifted to an applied anthropology approach in the 1970s and currently offers a master's degree in public archaeology. The public archaeology program combines the traditional research, science, methods, and theory in prehistory and historical archaeology with additional specialized class-work and an internship in aspects of public archaeology. Public archaeology is included in every archaeology course taught. A Ph.D. in public archaeology has been approved but still awaits funding and a new faculty line.

Boston University offers a master's program in archaeological heritage management through the Archaeology Department. The program offers specialized training for those who plan to pursue a career in CRM. It seeks to balance the academic study of archaeology with practical training in the identification, evaluation, and management of archaeological resources in the public interest. Although primarily focused on CRM in the U.S. context, the program is strongly grounded in international approaches to heritage management.

Obstacles to Change

Each of the authors has experienced frustration in trying to incorporate CRM and public archaeology into existing curricula or in attempting to develop new curricula. One obstacle to change has been faculty who often are unfamiliar with the complexities of the modern CRM profession and thus believe that the skills required for this work can best be learned on the job. Some academic archaeologists may consider the CRM profession as a marginal, second-class career track within the discipline for which they do not wish to train their students. Others may regard public archaeology as something to relegate to a class on CRM, rather than a holistic way of regarding the entire practice of archaeology.

Other obstacles encountered include lack of funding to support new programs; internal university decision making that places a higher priority on programs other than CRM; and politics at the statewide level that affect which colleges and universities get new programs and which programs are funded.

Elements of the Ideal Program

Below we attempt to list key elements that we identified as essential components of CRM/public archaeology training. They are in addition to the basic academic anthropological and archaeological background that all students should receive. Some of these elements can be incorporated easily into existing archaeology courses. Others will probably require new courses or different types of learning experiences.

• *Basic Archaeological Training.* Students need balanced training in current approaches to method and theory in both prehistoric and historical archaeology. Most CRM professionals will find themselves working with, and evaluating, both types of resources. Coursework and field experience involving both is essential.

• *Archaeological Fieldwork.* Archaeology students should receive basic experience in archaeological field and laboratory methods. This training is best obtained through a structured academic field school or by supervised participation on an archaeological field project.

• *Multidisciplinary Training.* Students will benefit from training in related disciplines, such as geology, geography, history, historic preservation, business, GIS and spatial analysis, archaeological conservation (artifacts), historic building conservation, landscape preservation, and preservation planning, as well as others. Interdepartmental relationships within institutions should be fostered to meet this need.

• *CRM Practice.* Students must learn how the legal and political systems work as they relate to cultural resource management and how the preservation system works at the local, state, and national levels. This information often is covered in a basic CRM course. It also is essential for students to receive practical experience in CRM projects. Academic programs could partner with CRM contractors to provide internships and other training and employment opportunities for their students. Students working on CRM projects should be apprised of the details of the overall project, and not just serve as crew members or laboratory workers. Experienced graduate students should be offered an opportunity to work in positions of responsibility.

We note with concern the lack of an up-to-date textbook on CRM and public archaeology.

• *Values and Ethics.* An essential component of any archaeologist's training must be a solid grounding in professional ethics. Students must learn, absorb, debate, and experience the central values of public archaeology (which is to say, of all archaeology): stewardship in the public interest; public and professional accountability; non-commercialization;

public education and outreach; and preservation. Students must be aware of the ethical dilemmas that are likely to face them in professional situations. And they must be able to articulate the value of cultural resources and archaeology to a variety of audiences and interests.

Students may become familiar with the ethical grounding of the profession in a course on professional ethics and values. Equally important, however, matters of ethics and professionalism should be a part of every archaeology course and field experience.

• *Communication Skills.* Effective communication is a critical element of CRM and public archaeology. Students must develop good written and verbal skills. They should be encouraged and required to write frequently for a variety of audiences; assignments might include academic papers, research grants, contract archaeology proposals, and articles geared for a popular audience. They should be encouraged to give oral presentations in their courses, professional lectures, and public lectures to school groups or interested organizations.

Numerous opportunities exist for giving students the opportunity to communicate with the diverse publics who have an interest in archaeology. Some examples include meeting with federal, state, and local elected officials and/or their staffs; attendance at a local planning meeting or a city council meeting; meeting with local Native Americans and other ethnic groups, property owners, and other local constituencies; visiting federal and state historic preservation offices; and attending meetings of local historic commissions, preservation boards, and museums.

Students also should develop an appreciation for the power of the press, the support that can be provided by the media, the problems of inaccurate and/or negative press coverage, and the methods that can be used to ensure accuracy in information. The media can be a valuable allies or sources of confusion. Students should learn how to write press releases and to think of positive media opportunities.

All these efforts to enhance our students' abilities to effectively convey the values and importance of public archaeology require a substantial commitment by both academic faculty and students. If our students are to be encouraged—even required—to speak to school groups, tourists, avocational societies, and others, there also must be a strong institutional commitment to this important dimension of public archaeology.

• *Management Skills.* Students should acquire basic management skills in planning, designing research plans, budgeting, setting up time-tables, and managing personnel. An archaeological seminar devoted to these topics would give prospective CRM graduates some much-needed experience in these areas. Advanced graduate students could run their own small contracts.

• •

Concluding Comments

Cultural resource management is a profession and, as such, requires its practitioners to receive specialized training in the skills that comprise the profession. Each of the authors in this section has attempted, within the constraints and particular circumstances of our individual programs—in departments of anthropology, history, and archaeology—to provide specialized training at the master's or doctoral level to our students so that they can become capable practitioners of CRM within an overall framework of public archaeology. We strongly believe in the need for specialized professional education for CRM archaeologists, but at the same time recognize that it may not be possible in every case to deliver the necessary training in the form of a separate, specialized degree program. However it is provided, we believe it is essential for the future of archaeology that the principles and practices of CRM and public archaeology be imparted, not just to students who plan to enter the CRM profession, but to all archaeology students.

References Cited

American Anthropological Association
1997 *American Anthropological Association 1997-98 Guide. A Guide to Programs. A Directory of Members.* American Anthropological Association, Arlington, Virginia.

Zeder, M. A.
1997 *The American Archaeologist: A Profile.* AltaMira, Walnut Creek.

Master's of Arts in Heritage Resources: A proposed program at Northwestern State University of Louisiana

Kathleen M. Byrd

U nlike the other programs discussed in this volume, all of which treat archaeology as the primary educational focus, the degree program described herein embeds archaeology in a curriculum that focuses on heritage resources. Northwestern State University (NSU) has had for a number of years a Cultural Resources Management option in its Master's of Arts in History program. Currently, NSU's faculty is halfway through the process of developing a Master's of Arts in Heritage Resources.[1] This new degree is designed to be multidisciplinary and would not be the best choice for someone who is interested strictly in archaeological research. Rather, it is devised for people who wish to approach heritage resources in a more holistic manner.

Goal

The goal of the Master's Program in Heritage Resources is to develop a highly motivated, knowledgeable, and skillful professional who, by working with groups and individuals, is able to develop integrated preservation strategies to protect and manage the total range of the country's heritage.

Objectives

To achieve this goal, NSU has identified four main objectives:
- to instill in the student a broad, knowledgeable, sympathetic understanding of preservation needs and an appreciation for the multiple elements of the nation's heritage resources;
- to equip each student with basic management and administrative skills in personnel management, budgeting, planning, scheduling, and program evaluations;
- to provide each student with specialized knowledge in at least one area of particular interest; and
- to develop the ability of each student to communicate persuasively, to negotiate different views, and to be a critical thinker and a problem solver.

Curriculum Outline

NSU's proposed program is divided into five parts, each designed to address one or more of the objectives listed above. The curriculum consists of a heritage resources component, a management component, an elective component, an internship, and a thesis.

Heritage Resources Component (15 credit hours)

The purpose of this component is to direct attention to primary research and preservation issues and techniques in the study of heritage resources and to encourage the integration of all relevant disciplines into the study of these resources: history, geography, anthropology/archaeology, and the built environment. For each of the principal disciplines in heritage resources, students will be required to take one course that concentrates on key research methods, theoretical approaches, and current issues. Research papers and oral presentations will be important elements in each course. Students will take one additional course designed to integrate these foundation courses, "Case Studies in Heritage Research." In this course, students will be required to select and study a site or area, and integrate the various disciplines in the development of a strategy for preserving and/or developing the site/area.

Management Component (6 credit hours)

The purpose of this component is to provide an opportunity for the student to learn basic administrative and problem-solving skills needed for any heritage resources program and to achieve an understanding of the laws, rules, and regulations affecting heritage resources preservation. Each student will take two courses. The first course will apply basic management concepts, such as human behavior and motivation techniques, budgeting, strategic planning, conflict resolution, consensus building, grantsmanship, grants management and fund raising, to heritage resource situations. The second course, "Cultural Resource Management," will consider the historic development of the heritage movement, its legal foundations, and the movement's main methods and conceptual bases.

Electives (12 credit hours)

The purpose is of this component is to allow the student to develop a professional focus to match his or her particular career goals. For example, a student who wishes to pursue a career with a federal agency working with Native American issues would be wise to select courses on public administration, preservation law, and Native Americans. Another student, whose career interests lie in public interpretation of the nation's past, might select museum and site development courses and several appropriate history courses. The range of choices in the elective area allows the student to tailor the degree program to meet individual long-range professional career goals.

Internship (3 credit hours)

The purpose of the internship is to provide students with direct experience in a governmental agency or on a heritage project. Each internship situation will be carefully and individually designed. The student, in conjunction with a faculty member and a representative from the agency or organization hosting the intern, will be responsible for conceptualizing a project, identifying the project goals and objectives, developing a work plan, and carrying the project to completion, including the writing and acceptance of the final report on the results.

Thesis (3-6 credit hours)

The purpose of the thesis is to demonstrate research competency, critical thinking skills, and problem-solving ability. The thesis will be a scholarly approach to solving a practical problem in heritage resources in an innovative way. Students will be encouraged to address problems facing agencies or heritage preservation professionals or to investigate issues that complement research being conducted by various local, state, and federal agencies.

Northwestern State University is fortunate in having several federal and state agencies in the Natchitoches area that are interested in cooperative programs with the university. Among these groups are the National Center for Preservation Technology and Training, the U.S. Forest Service, the Cane River Creole National Historic Park, the Cane River Heritage Area, the Louisiana Office of State Parks, Louisiana Creole Heritage Center, the Louisiana National Guard, local historic preservation organizations, and several historic house museums. Many of these organizations have expressed interest in hosting our student interns.

Current Status of the Program

When first proposed, the university asked a number of professionals in various areas to meet for a three-day workshop to discuss the elements that should be included in a heritage resources program. The results of this meeting were utilized in the development of the letter of intent that was approved by the university's management board and the Louisiana's higher education's policy board. The full proposal for this new degree program is under development.

Notes

[1]Heritage resources are the experiences of people as represented by a particular place and/or tradition. This term encompasses all the physical remains and oral traditions which contain significant information about the past. These include,

but are not limited to, features of prehistoric and historical archaeological sites; historic records, such as documents, diaries, and photographs; structures built in the past, such as houses, bars, and commercial buildings; objects, such as pottery and train locomotives; non-modified landscapes, such as prehistoric Indian ceremonial mound centers, rural agricultural fields, house gardens, and urban areas; industrial sites such as sawmills, sugar houses, and textile factories; and oral traditions, such as folk crafts, lore, and oral histories.

Cultural Resources Management at the College of William and Mary

Dennis B. Blanton

This paper explores some of the challenges in a program that attempts to address education in CRM/public archaeology through the informal vehicle of affiliation with an independently funded and staffed public archaeology facility. Such a program structure is by no means unique to the institution described here, William and Mary, and the educational implications that flow from it are undoubtedly shared across institutions as well. Even when a department recognizes the potential educational benefit of such an affiliation it can be difficult to forge a formal alliance, and students often are left to their own devices to pursue opportunities with the CRM affiliate until a structured program is implemented. A number of practical realities can impede the process of such a program's development regardless of the level of administrative interest and commitment. This example is offered to illustrate not only the complex issues but also to highlight potential solutions.

We need collectively to reflect on the educational implications of the assumption that students can learn how to do CRM/public archaeology on the job. What message do students receive about the importance of this work to the profession when this assumption informs the design of their curriculum? Is this message appropriate in the context of a profession that depends heavily on public funding for employment of its advanced degree recipients and for the underwriting of its research programs? Is it appropriate to maintain current *laissez-faire* curricular practices with both the content and our expectations for engagement with this key area of the discipline?

Background

The William and Mary Center for Archaeological Research (CAR) has been affiliated with the Department of Anthropology since the center was founded 11 years ago. The CAR was created with the principal purpose of meeting the local need for CRM services, but it also was recognized as a potential source of student support and training in the applied aspects of the discipline. The early years of its operation were necessarily focused on developing the consulting business rather than serving the needs of students, especially given the soft-money status of the operation.

After three or four years, the CAR staff turned more attention to developing an educational role to complement the service role. Up until that point, there was one CRM-oriented offering in the Department of Anthropology, taught by an adjunct faculty member as a survey course covering historic preservation law and process. In the absence of a formal component of the curriculum addressing contemporary public archaeology, the solution had been to modify courses with a guest lecture or a few outside readings. With more focused attention from CAR, attempts were made to alter this situation. CAR directors were provided with adjunct status, and an upper-level course was proposed to introduce students to the nuts and bolts of CRM archaeology. Acceptance of the CAR course proposal, "Practicing CRM Archaeology," demonstrated that affiliated consulting organizations can have an important role in an anthropology department's curriculum. The offering has been popular from the start and is now almost an unofficial requirement of M.A. students and committed, senior undergraduates concentrating on archaeology. The course has been offered once in each of the last 6 years and has been taught by CAR directors as an added responsibility with compensation returned to CAR to cover operating expenses.

At the same time, CAR created a summer internship program for M.A. students and senior undergraduates, designed to introduce two to five paid interns to the day-to-day practice of CRM. After about two months of field and laboratory time, the interns write a professional-quality technical report of their summer project. Here again, interns are trained as an extra responsibility of the CAR staff in the context of conducting full-time CRM consulting. The program also has become a popular one among students and, like the "Practicing CRM" class, the attraction is the very practical, marketable knowledge that is accrued in the process.

Several years ago, to augment the existing M.A. degree in historical archaeology, the CAR directors submitted a proposal for a formal M.A.-level track to prepare graduate students to function effectively in the CRM profession. A commitment for funding was secured from a state agency but the proposal was not executed. However, the Department of Anthropology has submitted a proposal for a Ph.D. in Historical Archaeology and Historical Anthropology with strong prospects for approval. Recognizing the need for CRM training, this proposal cites the CRM course and the potential internship opportunities through CAR as viable outlets.

Recent administrative changes have brought the role of CAR at William and Mary to the fore. An external review team examined its operation and recommended options for strengthening the CAR program, especially in the area of its potential curricular contributions. In essence, the reviewers recognized the tremendous potential for more formalized student involvement in CAR initiatives. Measures subsequently taken to strengthen the affiliation between the Department of Anthropology and CAR include the creation of a more active oversight board for CAR and college funding for a part-time liaison position. The liaison role of the new associate director for education at CAR is accomplished through active advocacy in the department, part-time teaching including the CRM course, and supervision of student research utilizing CAR project results.

Recognizing the Challenge

The CAR has grown into one of the region's leading CRM consulting operations. Regular, though limited, student opportunities are built into its CRM activities so that students can routinely volunteer or are employed on projects, and use the collections and facility for research. Independently, a summer internship program and a course in CRM archaeology are offered annually. These very positive, but still opportunistic, steps to accommodate student needs hardly exhaust the full potential for education through the affiliation of CAR and the Department of Anthropology. The question of interest is why attaining such a desirable goal has been so challenging.

Here, as elsewhere, there can be a significant generational factor informing decisions. Senior faculty often received the bulk of their professional experience pursuing more traditional brands of archaeology and as a result have not found it necessary or attractive to practice or teach in the CRM arena. While it is likely that senior faculty engaged in compliance studies during the earlier years of the national program, it remains the case that such activities were probably undertaken more to fill summer field schedules or to pursue occasional interesting research opportunities. For these reasons it is not unusual for senior faculty to overlook the complexity and demands of modern CRM practice and, thus, to underappreciate the critical need for professionally oriented training. When archaeology faculty expertise lies outside the United States, it also is sometimes difficult to build a strong appreciation for CRM training.

But faculty perspective is not the sole factor influencing program structure. Student demand is clearly at work in this arena as well. One aspect of student interest that may deflect attention from the role of public or applied issues in their education is the "romance of archaeology" or "carpe diem" factor driving many student decisions. The crux of the issue is that most students, even those committed to a career in archaeology, do not usually choose CRM as a focus while in school, given other opportunities for more traditional, exciting, or exotic experiences. These decisions are entirely understandable given the narratives that students are likely to have read about the history and conduct of the discipline. Nonetheless, their attraction to more satisfying, short-term options is one that matters to designers of professional programs in CRM/public archaeology. That the William and Mary program also can open the door for thrilling fieldwork at Colonial Williamsburg, Bermuda, the Caribbean, or Turkey means that few students will exercise the wisdom, willpower, or foresight to choose CRM training opportunities as summer fieldwork or CRM projects as the source for thesis topics. Moreover, students are rarely advised to make such choices, given the absence of a formal track in CRM archaeology (although the new liaison position at William and Mary is improving that shortcoming). Many, in fact, may actually be dissuaded from CRM options, partly as a result of the generational factor discussed above. Advisers also can easily convey, even if unconsciously, a second-class view of the "applied" rather than "pure research" nature of CRM studies.

It is time to examine this decision-making and advisement process more closely. Knowing full well that most jobs are in the CRM context or related government service, should not students—especially graduate students—be aggressively directed or advised towards CRM/public archaeology training? I refer here to programs that have a reasonable option to do so, such as a graduate program with an affiliated CRM contracting unit. Put another way, and again in the context of an appropriate setting, are we making the decisions that we feel are in the best career or professional interest of the students? Should they be allowed the freedom to design their own curriculum and emphasis? Or should CRM/public archaeology training be required in graduate programs? At William and Mary the latter question has been answered mainly by giving students a strong, basic foundation in archaeological method and theory, assuming that the skills required for a CRM position can be learned on the job.

Another challenge specific to the William and Mary case (although probably not unique in a structural context) relates to the level of support received by CAR. This CRM affiliate receives college support in the form of housing, a field vehicle, occasional office equipment such as computers, and most recently the funded, part-time liaison position. Otherwise, the CAR remains an entirely soft-money, contract-supported operation, although there are recent efforts to improve this status. What is important is the practical implications of this situation for stronger integration between the anthropology department and the affiliated contracting organization. The CAR is openly valued for the revenue it generates and applauded for the student support it has mustered, but its funding status prohibits further development of the educational mission. A persistent challenge, even with growing interest in developing CAR's educational role, has been to demonstrate that the shift in emphasis from service to education cannot occur without hard funding.

Making the Most of the Opportunities

Over the course of a decade the appreciation for the CAR at William and Mary has grown. There are now encouraging steps underway to integrate the program more fully with the educational mission of the college and balance its service role. The lessons learned can be valuable elsewhere and some recommendations are offered here to guide this process.

- Younger faculty with direct experience and training in CRM/public archaeology will enhance and foster a formal program of study in this area.
- Students will probably benefit most from a program that requires a minimal level of coursework and more internship-based training in CRM/public archaeology.
- CRM/public archaeology-oriented programs will be enhanced by an affiliated CRM contracting organization through which students can gain practical experience and research opportunities. The most effective operations will be supported by the institution for this role.
- CRM/public archaeology-oriented programs will be enhanced by a program that offers balanced exposure and training in the method and theory of prehistoric and historical archaeology.
- CRM/public archaeology-oriented programs will be enhanced by multidisciplinary training through interdepartmental relationships, so that courses in geology, geography, environmental sciences, and business can be arranged.
- Real opportunities exist for funding such training programs and internships at state agencies such as departments of transportation, private CRM firms, and major CRM customers such as energy/utility companies.
- A textbook outlined around agreed-upon minimum requirements for CRM/public archaeology training would aid our efforts considerably.

Nationally there is surely a limit to the number of programs that can effectively fill the need for CRM training. What this number may be remains to be seen; perhaps the market will serve to define the limit on its own. But given that there is likely to be such an upper limit, the profession should take note that a number of smaller schools, including junior colleges and vocational institutions, have considered and acted on the option of a program of "professional" archaeological training oriented to the CRM/public sector. It is not certain if this development is a good thing, especially knowing that the anthropological foundation in these curricula may be weak relative to larger programs. It is clearly now incumbent upon the profession to provide guidance aimed at ensuring quality in such programs.

This last point raises another important issue for the profession: Are some kind of national standards for CRM/public archaeology training advantageous, not only for the profession but also for the public who underwrites such a vast portion of the archaeological activity that takes place in the United States? Many professions require practitioners to meet minimal standards set by professional boards, and even require successful passage of an examination with periodic refreshers. This topic has been the focus of many active debates among CRM practitioners in recent years.

Finally, while much of this discussion has been directed towards graduate student training, it also is important to consider what kind of introduction undergraduates should be given to CRM/public archaeology. At William and Mary, advanced undergraduates are permitted to enroll in our CRM class and perform just fine. Moreover, the general consensus is that they find the class quite helpful, both in terms of skills acquisition and career planning (i.e., is CRM for me?).

In short, the William and Mary structure models a series of opportunities and challenges around the issue of designing undergraduate and graduate curricula in archaeology that meet more squarely the demands of a discipline that has a significant applied dimension. For those institutions that either have or are planning to follow a similar structure, one message is abundantly clear. The more informal the affiliation between a department and a public archaeology facility, the less likely it is that we will be able to meet student educational needs effectively. Arrangements that are in some measure more formalized are much clearer in depicting accurately for students the professional world in which they will operate.

A New Master's program in Archaeological Heritage management at Boston University

Ricardo J. Elia

A t Boston University, we have developed a new Master's program in archaeological heritage management through the archaeology department. Approved in January 1998, the program, is designed to offer specialized training for those who plan to pursue a career in cultural resource management (CRM). It seeks to balance the academic study of archaeology with practical training in the identification, evaluation, and management of archaeological resources in the public interest. Although the present program is primarily focused on cultural resource management in the United States, it is strongly grounded in international approaches to heritage management.

Rationale for a Program

We developed a concentration in public archaeology because we perceived a substantial gulf between the typical academic training of archaeologists and the actual practice of archaeology, especially as it has been affected by the emergence over the last three decades of a vast applied or public field, variously termed (although not strictly equivalent in meaning) cultural resource management archaeological heritage management, public archaeology, and contract archaeology. In my experience as the director of Boston University's Office of Public Archaeology, a university-based, cultural resource management unit, and as a faculty member in the archaeology department, archaeology graduates entering the cultural resource management field typically receive little or no specialized training for this career track. Their archaeological education, whether at the M.A. or Ph.D. level, was generally acquired in a traditional anthropology department and focused primarily on archaeological method, theory, and culture history. Many of these young professionals probably had some field experience working on CRM projects (generally as field or lab crew) and/or a course in CRM, but most were wholly unprepared to deal with the laws, procedures, policies, practice, and ethics of public archaeology.

It is difficult to quantify how much training in cultural resource management is offered in graduate programs, but several indications suggest a grim picture. In the 1997-98 *Guide of the American Anthropological Association*, which lists degree programs, faculty, and special programs offered by 430 academic departments of archaeology and anthropology in the United States, I counted only four undergraduate "certificate" programs in CRM or public archaeology and only four specialized M.A. degree programs (American Anthropological Association 1997). No wonder that many archaeologists working in public archaeology expressed "dissatisfaction with the adequacy of archaeologists' academic training as a preparation for their current careers. . .Clearly, many of these people feel strongly that the traditional academic training in archaeology is seriously out of step with the realities of archaeological practice in America today" (Zeder 1997:208).

Two decades ago, a "hands-on" approach to learning cultural resource management was perhaps an inevitable consequence of the emergence of a new mode of performing archaeology. Today, with a full-blown CRM bureaucracy and archaeological service industry, "learning by doing" is an unacceptable way of preparing young professionals and treating the archaeological heritage. The lack of specialized training is, in my opinion, one of the main reasons why the field of cultural resource management has been slow to mature in terms of professionalism since the 1970s, and why it seems to be regularly plagued by problems of standards, performance, and quality control.

Description of the M.A. Program

Students in the new program at Boston University are required to take eight courses for the M.A. Four are required: Intellectual History of Archaeology, Archaeological Ethics and Law, U.S. Archaeological Heritage Management; and a cultural resource management internship or practicum. In addition, students must take at least one course in archaeological science or technical study, and at least three courses in an archaeological concentration, such as historical archaeology or North American prehistory. Following completion of course requirements, a language requirement, and examinations, the student writes an M.A. thesis or report. Archaeological Ethics and Law, which is required of all graduate students in the department regardless of their specific degree program, introduces students to issues in archaeological professionalism, and treats archaeological ethics, the practice of archaeology, and the organization of archaeology in law on international, national, and local levels. (An undergraduate-level version of the same course also is available.) The course U.S. Archaeological Heritage Management is a detailed survey of legislation, regulations, procedures, and problems in the practice of U.S. public archaeology.

The practicum or internship provides practical experience in public archaeology for students. It typically involves up to three months of full-time, paid employment at an approved cultural resource management firm, state or federal agency, or other institution involved in the protection and management of archaeological heritage. The internship is considered an essential element of the M.A. concentration: it gives the student, following coursework, an opportunity to experience real-world employment responsibilities in cultural resource management. The student is not simply placed in a firm as field crew; instead, the student is expected to work on a substantial project that results in a CRM report or other assessable product. It generally is expected that the required M.A. thesis will be developed out of the student's internship project.

M.A. students in the heritage management concentration may select from a wide variety of courses in archaeology and related fields. Related departmental offerings include Topics in International Heritage Management; the first offering of this course studied CRM in the South Asian context and was taught by Rafique Mughal, the former antiquities director of Pakistan. Also offered in the archaeology department are graduate courses in conservation, geoarchaeology, GIS and spatial analysis, historical archaeology, paleoethnobotany, prehistoric North America, and remote sensing. Courses in other departments include a large number of offerings in preservation in the American and New England Studies Program, including New England preservation management, historic building conservation, introduction to landscape preservation, and introduction to preservation planning. Related courses are offered in the art history department and the School of Law.

Observations on the Program

Although the program was only approved in early 1998, the core courses have been in place for several years, and enough students have taken the essential elements of the concentration to allow some preliminary observations. One of the strongest points is the internship, which has provided strong practical (and paid) experience to five students to date. Three have worked for the Metropolitan District Commission, a Massachusetts agency responsible for extensive watershed lands that protect the state's drinking water supply. Documenting hundreds of archaeological sites in the watershed, students developed a management program to assist the agency in avoiding adverse outcomes to those sites during annual forest management activities (e.g., Fuchs 1994). Another student did two internships—one with the Boston Landmarks Commission, to develop a management plan to deal with historical gravestones displaced from the city's cemeteries (Erickson 1995), and the other with the R.S. Peabody Museum of Archaeology in Andover, Massachusetts, to work on a NAGPRA-related osteological analysis of skeletal remains excavated in 1925 to 1928 from the Etowah Site in Georgia (Erickson 1996). Another student completed an internship with the Trustees of Reservations, a private land trust in Massachusetts that acquires and preserves historical properties.

Many graduate students in other programs within the archaeology department, especially Ph.D. students concentrating in historical archaeology and North American prehistory, also participate in various aspects of the program. A few students are taking the M.A. in heritage management enroute to the Ph.D., anticipating that such a step will provide more practical experience and employment opportunities. Others are taking one or more of the cultural resource management courses without formally enrolling in the M.A. program.

At the same time, public archaeology and heritage management are not issues that are restricted to courses in the M.A. program. As members of an archaeology department, all of the faculty are actively involved in the professional and ethical issues central to the field, and students in all undergraduate and graduate classes are exposed to topics such as archaeology and the law; looting and the art market; professional ethics; reburial and repatriation; and site preservation and management.

A few potential problems with the program structure have arisen. One of the most serious is that students who concentrate on cultural resource management in an eight-course M.A. have little time to develop a specialty in a more traditional area of archaeology, such as historical archaeology. We are attempting to address that problem by admitting students into the program who already have strong undergraduate-level backgrounds in archaeology or anthropology, or by expecting M.A. students to rectify any deficiencies they may have in their previous training. Another concern is that the M.A. level should not be seen as the endpoint for professional training in cultural resource management and public archaeology.

Although many departments interested in developing similar specialized training programs are likely to encounter difficulties even at the M.A. level, I believe it is both inevitable and thoroughly desirable that universities offer a public archaeology specialization at the Ph.D. level. Certainly it is incumbent on graduate programs to develop the highest levels of intellectual and technical skills in young professionals, since many of them will pursue careers in cultural resource management. Moreover, inasmuch as publicly supported projects fund a major segment of the archaeological research conducted in the United States today, then certainly it is the responsibility of the discipline to educate the young professionals likely to practice in this arena to the highest research standards. It is only through such an approach to the graduate curriculum that we will be assured that public funding will underwrite the generation of valuable new knowledge about the past.

References Cited

American Archaeological Association
1997   *American Archaeological Association 1995-1996 Guide: A Guide to Departments. A Guide to Members.* American Anthropological Association, Arlington, Virginia.

Erickson, H. A.
1995   "Historic Gravestone Fragments: A Collections Management Plan," *Northeast Historical Archaeology* 24:9-18.

1996   *Skeletal Analysis of Individuals from the Etowah Site, Georgia: Remains Excavated by W.K. Moorehead, 1925-1928.* Unpublished Master's thesis, Boston University.

Fuchs, A. J.
1994   *Documentary Survey and Inventory of Historical Archaeological Resources on the Prescott Peninsula, Quabbin Reservoir.* Report of Investigations No. 133. Office of Public Archaeology, Boston University.

Zeder, M. A.
1997   *The American Archaeologist: A Profile.* AltaMira Press, Walnut Creek.

Teaching Public Archaeology at the University of South Florida

Nancy Marie White

Following national trends in anthropology and also for purposes of institutional viability, the Department of Anthropology at the University of South Florida (USF) successfully shifted its focus in the 1970s to applied anthropology, which was understood naturally to include public archaeology. Thus, USF became the first department in the United States to award graduate degrees (M.A. and Ph.D.) in applied anthropology, including an M.A. in Public Archaeology (the approved archaeology Ph.D. still awaits funding and another faculty line). The public archaeology training includes all the traditional elements of a research-focused degree program, including method and theory, archaeological science, fieldwork, prehistoric and historic archaeology, but with the addition of specialized coursework in all aspects of public archaeology. We are now ethically obliged to include public archaeology in every academic archaeology course. As we produce more professional archaeologists, not to mention civil engineers, environmental specialists, and social and natural scientists, we must include in their training the understanding that *all* archaeology is public archaeology, and that we need to preserve the human past for practical as well as esoteric reasons.

The public is always involved with archaeological practice in some way. Most of our research is supported by public funding and/or required by public law. Much of our knowledge of archaeological site locations and histories comes from local people. Labor-intensive as archaeology is, today many field and lab projects cannot be accomplished without lay volunteers. More and more archaeological sites are being mined by people seeking the fun (and increasing profit) of collecting artifacts. The news media crave stories that shed light on the human past and reflect upon the modern human condition. The largest audience for our archaeological product is the general public, who are fascinated with the romance of the past and desire to learn about it. Each archaeologist must be prepared not only to deal with but to embrace the public, and to be a teacher of archaeology and preservation as part of the everyday job.

What is Public Archaeology?

In many programs, the incorporation of public archaeology into the professional training curriculum is limited to explaining cultural resource management (CRM) or including students in contract archaeology projects; this is woefully inadequate preparation for interaction with

Native Americans, schoolchildren and their teachers, taxpayers, news reporters, legislators, hobbyists, land developers, art dealers, corporate decisionmakers, and/or various public officials. At USF, we consider public archaeology to include the following:

- anthropological understanding of Native American issues, as well as those of other cultural groups whose ancestral material culture and skeletal remains one might encounter and study in the process of doing archaeology
- archaeological ethics
- archaeology in the communications media, from news reporting to portrayal in popular culture such as books, movies, computer games, and the Internet
- avocational archaeologists and associations, collectors' societies, looting vs. pothunting vs. amateur archaeology (including underwater)
- both CRM and contract archaeology (which are very different things)
- general public understanding of the value of archaeology, of collecting and looting, especially as compared with other kinds of illegal activities
- U.S. historic preservation law; the National Register and the concept of significance; federal, state, and local bureaucratic systems and legislative processes, including lobbying, legislative history, current government affairs
- international antiquities laws, including the 1970 UNESCO cultural property convention and other international agreements
- international cultural heritage management programs, including divergence from law to practice and public attitudes in different countries
- museology; exhibits preparation and interpretation
- practical applications of archaeological knowledge in dealing with modern human problems, from natural resource exploitation to schemes for long-term storage of nuclear waste
- hosting an archaeology day, week, or month program
- site preservation methods: physical, legal, private, and public
- speaking to various public audiences, from schoolchildren to lawyers to elderhostel groups
- writing for the public
- writing/presenting popular summaries of specific research, even of thesis projects

Public Audiences for Archaeology

The general public is interested in and often fascinated with archaeology. Students' training must prepare them to respond to this interest wherever it is encountered. No archaeologist can be a professional without having had to speak in a classroom or museum to children, tourists, avocational archaeologists, or other audiences. There are now many tools to aid in this process. Clear speech and hands-on, attractive artifacts are essential. One can make teaching kits and displays tailored to the audience and/or geared to local history, prehistory, or modern garbology; suggest vacation travel or Internet websites; wear archaeology t-shirts; show exciting slides; and publicize state archaeology day/week/month programs. Students also must learn how to convey the politics of archaeology and preservation (Whose voices are presented in the display? Whose sites are conserved?), promote cultural diversity and science education, and show the practical value of learning from the past. The "archaeology day" program is ideal for information exchange between archaeology students and the lay public, and can be easily programmed in one's own research area.

As students develop these skills, they come to realize that the profession *needs* the public, whether for funding, finding and excavating sites, or saving sites.

Historic Preservation, Law Enforcement, CRM, Contract Archaeology

These are all different arenas for accomplishing archaeology, and the student must learn about each to attain an awareness of where they do and do not overlap. Hiring students to conduct contract surveys is not enough, and contract archaeology is not CRM. Students should be able to run their own small contracts and should learn the preservation system that provides context for this work. They should visit federal and state historic preservation offices, learn about local community preservation boards and museums, study physical preservation techniques, learn laws, meet or communicate with legislators and lobbyists. They should be assigned to write both research grant and contract archaeology proposals and meet in the classroom with resource managers, contract archaeologists, Native Americans, customs agents, and other appropriate individuals. Basic aspects of these professionals' jobs, including antiquities laws, business practices, the changing concept of archaeological significance, ethics, looters, money and accounting, Native Americans and other ethnic groups, politics at every level, and skeletal remains, should be discussed within an anthropological perspective.

This kind of training teaches students that "pure" research does not exist, and that archaeology will be hard to do if the resource is not preserved or accessible. Courses in the philosophy of archaeology and critical theory need to make students aware that although postprocessual prose, marxist hypothesizing, or Binfordian scientific jargon may frame how we think about the past within the discipline, most archaeological interpretation today is accomplished by those who present it to the public and thoroughly understand all the different entities that constitute the public. This latter work needs to be examined alongside the former in such courses.

Writing for the Public

Reaching the public with words is not hard if one throws out the dense prose of academic archaeology and CRM reports and remembers that "specialized resource procurement station" is really "hunting camp" and that the "trajectory of lithic manufacture" is the "way they chipped stone tools." On the other hand, most children (and lay adults) love to learn more accurate scientific terms such as "projectile point" or "coprolite." Students can learn to convey their own sense of the magic and mystery of archaeology to attract and educate the public. Universities offer support classes in good writing and speaking. Education classes are helpful to prepare for audiences of schoolchildren. Archaeology students also can learn public education through taking museology classes, creating exhibits, and even providing interpretive displays associated with contract and compliance projects.

The Public Media

Understanding archaeology in the popular media—from newspaper stories to Indiana Jones—is easy. Today's archaeology students have grown up with Fred Flintstone riding dinosaurs and Lara the Tomb Raider in video games. They already know how to counter the messages in these popular stereotypes. It is trickier to teach them to deal with media attention in their own work and to be sure that it is beneficial to both the research and the public. Advance preparation of press releases and photos works well, as does helping them anticipate what different news media want to do and know, discussing ethics and the disclosure of site locations to reporters, and reminding them to acknowledge and thank supporters. The idea is to find common ground with those bringing the news to the public: agreement that our common heritage expressed in the archaeological record is being saved and studied.

Avocational Archaeology and Public Programs

Avocational groups are the secret weapons for protecting sites, as Hester Davis has said (1991). They also are sources of research data and support, and wonderful for both learning and teaching public archaeology. These groups are the most interested, self-selected members of the public. Archaeologists must join them, give talks, gain volunteers for field or lab work. Many state humanities councils support public participation in workshops, archaeology day/week/month programs, and field projects. Incorporating local residents into field or lab projects can turn looters and ethical collectors alike into good public archaeologists. Archaeology students need to become successful emissaries to the avocational community; many started out there themselves.

The Popular Audience, the Undergraduate Student, and the Ultimate Ethical Responsibility

The public is not only essential to individual research, it also is a necessary component of ethical archaeology. For this reason public archaeology should be incorporated in some way into every graduate/professional archaeology course, not to mention other anthropology classes. Every good introductory anthropology text now has something on CRM and historic preservation. Instructors should expand this to include at least a small representation of the diverse aspects of public archaeology, from saving a site threatened by a new shopping mall, to the recent news controversy about "Kennewick Man," to why the latest Hollywood movie on archaeology has some inaccuracies. If we build a strong understanding of key issues at the undergraduate level, we can expect to accomplish more sophisticated outcomes more efficiently at the graduate level.

Getting the message out is important simply as a central, if not ultimate goal of social science research. As we move from knowledge to wisdom in the profession, we absolutely must realize the importance of going beyond even the most fascinating research and applying the lessons of the human past. As we focus our students' attention on interpreting the meaning of our work to the public, the archaeological record's potential for offering insights into modern problems, from global to local, is clarified for the professional as well as the lay audience.

Conclusion

These themes and concerns can be accommodated within any archaeology program, from specialized curricula, such as the one at USF, to general classes. Archaeology training must produce professionals well versed in the variety of demands that they are likely to encounter in the realm of public archaeology, and it is critical that graduate programs begin to explore how they might achieve this goal within their current structure. Likewise, we practicing archaeologists and teachers must become students once again, either formally or self-directed, with assistance from professional organizations if needed, to gain an understanding of public archaeology that will permeate and enhance all our work.

References Cited

Davis, H. A.
1991 Avocational Archaeology Groups: A Secret Weapon for Site Protection. In *Protecting the Past,* edited by G. S. Smith and J. E. Ehrenhard, pp. 175-80. CRC Press, Boca Raton.

V.

Questioning
the principles

INTRODUCTION:
THINKING OUTSIDE THE BOX

In this section, the findings, principles, and recommendations of the Task Force on Curriculum are discussed and evaluated by individuals representing diverse segments of the archaeological community. Although there is a healthy variety of opinion, there is considerable common ground. It is clear that the demands of the profession have changed considerably in the latter part of the twentieth century, and that the requirements of professional practice are not always addressed by the curricula at most of our academic institutions. Changes at the undergraduate, graduate, and postgraduate levels are clearly called for. These changes are best implemented at the departmental level through curriculum reform and effective teaching, and they should make use of pedagogical methods that take advantage of advanced technologies such as the Internet.

Although the education of the next generation of archaeologists will take place in the context of curricula designed by academic faculty, the perspectives of the private and governmental sectors need to be reflected in these curricula, as do the demands of the diverse communities that archaeologists serve. As more and more decisions concerning archaeology and archaeologists are being made by those outside the discipline, the profession and its practitioners must be able to function in and respond appropriately to this environment. These are issues that can find their way creatively into the knowledge and skills base that teacher/scholars develop with their students throughout the undergraduate and graduate years. To this end, a set of ethical principles can provide an overall context and direction for change as it is incorporated systematically and thoughtfully into graduate and undergraduate curricula. The following papers by K. Anne Pyburn (academic sector), Brian Fagan (academic sector), Joseph Schuldenrein (private sector), and David Anderson (governmental sector) bring their perspectives to these issues.

Altered States:
Archaeologists under siege
in Academe

K. Anne Pyburn

When Alison Wylie writes that archaeology is in the middle of a paradigm shift, her words sound exhilarating. Her argument makes me feel like I'm on the cutting edge of a science that is making changes—changes in itself as a scholarly discipline, and changes in the world that archaeologists effect as scientists bent on important discovery. I think she is correct but that she may understate the situation of our altered state as a discipline; the truth is that we are under siege.

Like any other academic discipline we are short of funding; most of us predicted that a demographic surge would occur right about now just as our mentors were beginning to retire and the job market would open up for our underemployed colleagues and our recent PhDs. What we are seeing instead is that although more students are showing up at many universities and many senior faculty are retiring, universities are shutting down lines and hiring junior people or no one at all. The economy is good, federal and local governments have surpluses, but education is taking it on the chin—especially "frivolous" liberal arts programs like anthropology that demonstrably do not lead to jobs in anthropology. Attempts to capture academic effort with characterizations that suit the modern fiscal climate would be hilarious if they were not so disturbing. In a recent newspaper interview, one of the trustees of my university referred to academic departments as "degree production units."

There also is a lack of funding for basic research. The National Science Foundation continues to add increments to its offering, but I was shocked to find that archaeology receives less support than linguistics at the federal level. Anthropological linguistics graduated two PhDs in the whole of the United States last year (1998). The National Endowment for the Humanities (NEH), after being gutted by Congress a few years ago, has never returned to the level of support it once offered archaeologists.

As our jobs and our research shrink, we nevertheless are increasingly in the news, and not as crusaders for good. As Native peoples seek human rights and self-determination, the colonialist past of archaeology threatens to overwhelm and undermine modern research. Native Americans in ever-increasing numbers criticize archaeology as soulless and selfish, exploitative and hegemonic, disrespectful and evil. Europeans and Euro-Americans often are the most negative when they speak on behalf of first peoples; last year I read a statement by a colleague in philosophy arguing that the archaeological analysis of human remains is the moral equivalent of Nazi medical experimentation on living people in death camps.

Looters, of course, have no standards of political correctness. During the Afghanistan civil war, when armies overran the national museum at Kabul, soldiers were armed with museum catalogues given to them by collectors who had circled the objects of their desire. The museum was looted by soldiers with shopping lists. The palace of Asubanipal in Iraq also is disappearing as we discuss the issues at hand. And perhaps this is better than what bombs do in the wars raging in many parts of the world.

Today $1.1 trillion, the equivalent of the income of the bottom 52 percent of people in the world, is owned by 447 individuals. The inequity of this situation is almost incomprehensible; clearly such wealth places some people above the law and places decisions about the distribution of resources that have life-and-death consequences in the hands of individuals who have no accountability. The terrible power and jaded sensibilities of such people lead to all sorts of excess, so collecting artifacts seems almost benign in this context. Nevertheless, it is clear that no amount of moralizing can touch this sector of humanity and acquisition will continue to be attractive as long as there are things to acquire. The rarer the material, the more desirable a collection it makes for the super rich. I recently ran across a Web page where a Neanderthal skull was offered for sale by a young man who had "inherited" it from his grandfather and was selling it to finance his college education.

Closer to home, many of us are fighting what some of my colleagues call "culture wars." Because science has served dubious political ends and biased research goals have sullied the history of social science, anthropologists have come to question whether we can do science at all. Some of the finest departments in the United States have split into factions over this issue and then proceeded to divide into separate departments. When the smoke clears, archaeology usually falls onto the side of unthinking brute positivism, at least according to those standing on the other side. Regardless of which side, if either you support, this sort of divisiveness cannot help us in a world that already suspects us of irrelevance and intellectual self-indulgence.

And within our own ranks, our analysis of ourselves is none too flattering. Positions of power and authority in archaeology are still overwhelmingly in the hands of Euro-American men. There are more women with successful careers in archaeology than there were 20 years ago, but fewer than many of us thought before Melinda Zeder (*The American Archaeologist*) produced the figures. The number of women in archaeology who have tenured (or even tenure line) faculty positions and research grants is astonishingly small, in this day when our female students no longer even know what feminism is. The percentage of archaeologists who are people of color is minute. This situation complicates our ability to present a convincing case that the archaeological record belongs not to any single group but to all humanity.

Into this context, we bring idealistic undergraduates and determined, passionate graduate students. Almost none of them have any idea of what they will face with a degree in anthropology or archaeology. Many academics, once considered the preferred position for an archaeologist, are engaged in an immediate struggle for individual survival: keeping departments open, finding minimal research funding, publishing rapidly enough to stay on the tenure track, meeting federal requirements and the concerns of living people who have an interest in our research areas. Retooling our university curricula has not been high on our list of chores.

Nevertheless, all of us have some level of commitment to education, and for most of us it is a passion. And most archaeologists are accustomed to an empirical approach to understanding. What the facts and figures show is that we are failing to prepare our students to take up jobs in archaeology in the present world, even when those jobs are offered. The world has changed, our discipline has changed, our students have changed, our curricula must change. These academic changes are not mandated by the reduced capacity of a dumber set of students, as I have heard some colleagues claim, or lessened expectations for academic positions, although those are scarce. They are mandated for the survival of our discipline and the preservation of the archaeological record.

The Society for American Archaeology has decreed stewardship as our highest priority and our ethical responsibility as academics can no longer be discharged with a couple of public lectures and a newspaper interview. We have to teach our students how to face collectors, looters, angry Native peoples, fiscally strapped deans, search committees, and wily land developers, which means we have to figure out how to do this ourselves. And we cannot continue to extol simplistic notions of human history that unwittingly elevate the contribution of Europeans and lay all human progress at the feet of men; there are human consequences of this sort of perspective, and it is time for us to realize that is possible to be rigorously empirical and still leave sexism and racism in the past. Viable archaeologists of the next millenium must be able to test the theoretical propositions of Appadurai, Gramschi, Miller, and Muckerji with concrete data that rule out competing hypotheses.

Once upon a time, when all archaeology jobs required a Ph.D. because they were in some way under the control of universities, a master's degree was for students who were considered second rate, and not even essential to the pursuit of a Ph.D. Often a master's was simply a matter of a bit of bureaucratic paperwork filled out along the way to a Ph.D., requiring a certain set of classes and number of hours, but no thesis and no particular demonstration of competence. Consequently, many departments granted what came to be known as a terminal master's degree—given to students who were not destined to go on to become real archaeologists.

The rise of contract archaeology and government jobs has radically changed this picture. Successful archaeologists working outside academia control far more money than academics and the bulk of research in the United States is in their control. Many of these archaeologists do not have and do not need a Ph.D., and many of them feel, quite rightly, that their academic background that did not treat a master's candidate as a serious student or a potential professional, was a waste of their time, a credential with no content.

This is clearly a shameful situation. The master's degree is currently our major professional degree, and must, if anything, require *more* rigor and emphasis on competency than the Ph.D. Members of the task force all agreed strongly that master's degrees should almost never be awarded without requiring a thesis.

Please do not think that the SAA Task Force on Curriculum believes it has solved these problems or has arrogant plans to mandate a brave new academic world. Although we were all passionate in our commitment to our discipline, we disagreed about which changes to recommend and their implementation. But in the end we agreed strongly on a number of principles. Having described the crisis that has led to these resolutions, I hope I have convinced you to study this publication and respond seriously and constructively.

strategies for change in teaching and learning

Brian M. Fagan

S tewardship, diverse pasts, social relevance, ethics and values, written and oral communication, basic archaeological skills, and real world experience. There seems to be little disagreement as to the broad context of our discussions. But where do we go from here? The comments that follow offer some thoughts and potential action items.

Undergraduate Education
Introductory Courses

Most of our beginning students come to us with little awareness of archaeology. Many are totally indifferent to the subject. Here we meet the general public, and have the mission not of training professional archaeologists, but of creating an informed citizenry.

I think the most important ingredients in a beginning class are ones that can only be brought to the subject by the instructor: an infectious enthusiasm and passion for the past, a belief that archaeology has great relevance to the contemporary world, a deep-felt interest in students as individuals and human beings, and, above all, electric story-telling skills, the ability to explain eloquently how archaeology works.

In other words, those who teach beginning archaeology must care passionately about TEACHING and their students. I write TEACHING in capitals, for it is all-too-often considered as a second-rate pastime when compared with the Great God Research or other professional activities.

Action Item. If there is one way to improve peoples' appreciation of archaeology, it is to foster the importance of experienced, passionate teachers in the classroom. As a profession, we have done little to make teaching one of our highest, if not our highest, priority. We need a powerful, profession-wide commitment to good teaching and training.

However, we have to train these teachers properly. Not only must they be masters of pedagogy, they must have a broad grasp of the global past. Please realize we are talking about ALL of archaeology at this level, not just North America. Can you imagine an introductory course on archaeology that does not cover Olduvai Gorge, Tutankhamen, and the Lords of Sipan? If you want to teach about diverse pasts, you cannot ignore other parts of the world. In these days of over-specialization, many people teach with overly narrow intellectual blinkers.

I think most of us do a pretty good job of informing beginning students about stewardship, the social importance of archaeology, and the meaning and finite nature of the archaeological record. They have been implicit realities of lower-division teaching for a generation. Judging from conversations with many colleagues, topics like diverse perspectives on the past, the ethics of living responsibly with the archaeological record, and gender are percolating rapidly into many beginning courses.

We are urged to train people in oral presentation and writing skills. Anyone who uses a multiple-choice test in a lower-division university course should be shot. This is where the quest for better literacy begins. A new generation of multimedia technologies allow us to tackle this problem in new and creative ways.

> ***Action item.*** **Develop and disseminate learning materials and case studies on specific topics in the "renewed archaeology curriculum" for incorporation in beginning courses.**

I cannot stress too strongly that it is pedagogically naive to think that the creation and dissemination of some standard and complete introductory course packages, however innovative, will be an important step forward. A vast literature in instructional development has long shown the folly of this approach, which simply does not work.

Upper-Division Undergraduates

Here's another reality to bear in mind. Only a tiny proportion of upper-division undergraduates eventually become professional archaeologists, although many may retain a lifelong interest in the subject. Upper-division courses cater, for the most part, to people who are going on to worlds far from archaeology. Again, we are creating an informed citizenry, albeit in smaller numbers, but this time at a more intensive level.

In my view, upper-division courses should be predominantly intellectual in their content, while emphasizing basic literacy and critical skills. By their nature, advanced method and theory courses and area offerings cover a wide range of archaeological topics and interests and deal with many basic skills. Such courses provide an admirable context for discussing ethical issues, professional values, and real-world problem solving, using actual archaeological data. However, specific teaching materials in these general areas are thin on the ground.

Perhaps even more important is achieving a much more sophisticated understanding of Native American culture and history among anthropology majors. At the moment, most students graduate with almost no awareness of this all-important subject.

Action item. Make a systematic effort to create a wide range of "real-world" case studies that deal with ethical, professional, and decision-making issues, using data from many regions. These modules should be directed, in particular, at advanced method and theory courses.

Action item. Add a major component of Native American studies to upper-division curricula.

I think this kind of intellectual, upper-division curriculum is ideal, even for the small numbers of undergraduates who want to pursue archaeological careers. I firmly believe that responsibility for learning lies with the student, that anyone seriously interested in archaeology as a career will seek out instructors or working archaeologists and actively look for internship and fieldwork experiences, many of them in the cultural resource management (CRM) world. It is here that encouragement and mentorship play a vital role.

Action item: Encourage mentorship of undergraduates with a serious career interest outside academia. The major initiatives here lie with the private and public sectors. Have, for example, the latter explored the option of giving scholarships to promising students as they enter graduate school?

Graduate Education and Training

Without question, most of the education and training concerns outlined by the Task Force on Curriculum lie at the graduate level. Here we confront a powerful reality, which extends far beyond the narrow confines of archaeology: most graduate programs are predominantly intellectual, for they are in the business of training academic archaeologists—Ph.D.s. There are plenty of master's programs around the country, but, with notable exceptions, many of them are still predominantly intellectual. Survey data tells us many departments do not have the resources or the trained faculty to teach the topics covered in the "Renewed Archaeology Curriculum." In some cases, too, there is still a pervasive attitude that non-academic archaeology is inferior. It is unbelievable that this bankrupt dogma still haunts academia. Changing this mind set must be a high priority for the future, and can only done by proper graduate education and training, encouragement of the young, and constant dialogue among archaeologists of all persuasions. This dialogue has already begun, and is manifested in some important research in the academic literature. But we still have a long way to go.

Action Item. **From the beginning, reinforce the principle that, whatever changes we make in graduate teaching, a sound
and sophisticated intellectual grounding in both
archaeology and Native American studies is vital to
every professional North American archaeologist,
whatever their career path.**

Professional training in archaeology at the graduate level is long
overdue for a massive overhaul, and this is where the major curricular
changes lie. At issue here is the need for in-depth training and practical
experience for people planning careers in the public or private sectors, in
non-academic settings, where a diversity of skills are needed. As has been
pointed out, the master's degree is the most appropriate qualification for
entry into the nonacademic world, for the Ph.D. is a pure research
degree. Most M.A.s are still predominantly academic, simply because most
graduate curricula are aimed, ultimately, at Ph.D. students, whose
concerns are narrowly academic. While some institutions already offer
innovative and successful M.A. programs in topics such as historic preservation and public archaeology, a strong case can be made for the development of more highly selective M.A. programs, which train professional
leaders for the new millennium.

Action Item. **Encourage the development of a series of innovative,
multidisciplinary M.A. programs at geographically separated institutions aimed specifically at training people
for nonacademic archaeological careers. The public and
private sector should be actively involved in such
programs as part of the teaching and internship process. Such encouragement could take the form of offering consulting advice, pooled experience, and so on.**

What North American archaeology really needs is a few top-flight
professional schools to train people for the nonacademic sector, such as
one finds for environmental management, law, and so on. However, this
is a very expensive option, whereas many administrators will be attracted
to the relatively low-cost alternative of a multidisciplinary program. But
the development of such programs requires real commitment from the
faculty and nonacademic archaeologists involved, a key issue when
considering strategies for academic change.

A final point on graduate education. In-service and continuing
education are becoming a career-long reality for nonacademic archaeologists. To what extent do "training on the job" and such skill-related
courses, often offered in the contact of a work environment, take the load
off graduate programs? This issue needs in-depth exploration.

But again I reiterate: the future of archaeology depends as much on sound intellectual training as it does specific professional skills.

Action Items. **Develop models and specimen curricula for M.A. programs aimed at nonacademic archaeologists, also course designs and modules, which could amplify an academic curriculum at minimal cost.**

Develop clear distinctions between beginning graduate training needs and those acquired by specific skills development courses later.

Closely define the roles that can be played by nonacademic archaeologists in master's programs in highly specific terms, for curriculum and course development purposes.

Strategies for Academic Change

People outside academia tend to be astoundingly naive about instructional innovation. Thus, we must never forget that curriculum and course changes lie, ultimately, with university and college faculty, however persuasive administrators may be. Without faculty leadership, commitment, and enthusiasm, curriculum change in archaeology is dead in the water. It is naive to think that academic archaeologists will embrace new curricular proposals or packaged courses when they are basically happy with their present courses and curricula. As any dean of undergraduate education will tell you, head-on suggestions for curriculum reform just do not work, especially in circumstances where faculty can claim that they already address many of the suggested innovations already—as many in archaeology will.

I also reiterate: standardized courses, as packages, will never work, largely because individual teachers have their own agendas and priorities. If our experience at UC-Santa Barbara is any guide, most people will use only small portions of a standardized course—and they may not be the parts the developers want them to use. You can be sure that if standardized courses worked, the commercial publishers would have produced them years ago. All their efforts to do so have failed, whereas short, computer-based modules and CDs have enjoyed some success.

The most successful strategies for long-term instructional change begin by working with individual faculty: provide them with funds; supply specific, example-related instructional materials and other facilities; help them in instructional design; and evaluate their courses, then propagate their success. This subtle, highly directed approach of proven effectiveness will yield rich dividends in the long run, but not instant gratification. It permits diversity, encourages interest in change, and rewards success.

Please do not reinvent the pedagogical wheel: the strategies for promoting instructional change are well developed and widely published. Work with committed individuals and institutions by providing specific materials, funding, and evaluation backup.

Action Item. **Focus efforts not on entire courses or curricula, but suggesting potential design and delivery strategies and on providing highly specific instructional materials that can be made available widely at rock-bottom cost.**

The Issue of Delivery

We stand on the threshold of a major revolution in higher education, where the World Wide Web enables us to deliver top-flight instructional materials virtually instantaneously to any place on earth. It is a matter of time before institutions collaborate on courses of all kinds, where instructors thousands of miles away from one another contribute to one another's courses, and where students in Oshkosh learn alongside those in New Zealand. I am surprised to find virtually no mention of this impending revolution in the documents prepared by the Task Force on Curriculum. The Web offers absolutely unlimited opportunities for changing undergraduate and graduate curricula everywhere, not by delivering standard courses, but providing high-quality instructional materials on specific topics to everyone.

Herein lies the best opportunity for curricular reform. If our experience at UC-Santa Barbara is any guide, there is open-ended demand for computer-based problems, specific instructional materials, and other learning resources that lie outside the immediate expertise of an instructor. Today, there is no need to buy publishers' standardized packages: you can download the material from the Web. The technology is proven, reliable, and very cheap.

Action item. **Use the proven medium of the World Wide Web to disseminate instructional materials to the archaeological community at rock-bottom cost.**

Textbooks

Textbooks are market-driven. Their content reflects what instructors around the country and the world teach in their beginning courses. An extensive review process of any textbook manuscript ensures that the resulting book is in tune with what is going on in the marketplace. As an active textbook author, I would say that all the basic books on the market do a very fair job of presenting the reality of contemporary archaeology to beginning students. We are sometimes accused of not giving a fair shake to CRM and not covering the topics advocated here. To my knowledge, at least one introductory text has had a stand-alone chapter on all aspects of CRM since 1981, while basic ethics, the finite nature of the record, and the relevance of archaeology have been important topics since the 1960s. What we are really concerned with here is some upper-division and graduate training where specific modules delivered by the Web would be highly effective.

I am sure that the marketplace will give birth to textbooks on nonacademic archaeology of all kinds within a very short time, once the demand for relevant courses is there. Indeed, I believe they are under contract. But for many of the topics in the "renewed archaeology curriculum," the Web offers much greater possibilities.

Finally, I suspect that we have significant momentum. The forces of the marketplace will lead to many important changes in undergraduate and graduate curricula. Allow these forces to work. If good, multidisciplinary M.A. programs for nonacademics come into being and offer open-ended career opportunities, they are bound to expand at the expense of more conventional academic programs and reduce the current overproduction of Ph.D.s, which must be near 60 percent to 80 percent over need in some specialties. Then you will see rapid curriculum change even at the most ardent research institutions.

But, above all, encourage people to teach, to innovate in the classroom. Without their individual and collective commitment, you are shouting into the wind.

Refashioning our profession: practical skills, preservation, and cultural resource management

Joseph Schuldenrein

It is clear that revamping is required at all stages of the archaeological education process. However, it is equally apparent that many changes can and will be made irrespective of our own good intentions and broad idealistic visions of a "better archaeology." If nothing else, our own experiences as professionals—from young students to seasoned professionals—has taught us that a combination of our own principles and the realities of the marketplace will result in the transformation of our profession. We have a strong potential to engineer that transformation, but only if we keep our vision strong and our empirical senses honed. We need to have principles, but not be quixotically headstrong; we must clamor for reform that can be implemented within the global realities of the twenty-first century. I am not arguing for dampening of principles, but rather for sharpening our visions—and more significantly—to mesh with the changing function of archaeology in the new millennium. The downside is that if we do not exhibit sufficient flexibility and political savvy in the upcoming years, decisions will be made for us and not by us. History teaches this lesson all too well.

The most critical lesson for archaeologists concerns our perception of the profession's progress in the past 30 years. If I were to poll all archaeologists about the single most significant development in archaeology for this period, I assume fewer than 10 percent would mention the environmental movement of the mid to late 1960s. Its momentum resulted in the National Environmental Protection Act (NEPA) and the National Historic Preservation Act (NHPA). Ultimately it spawned the archaeology boom, one which has produced what is hopefully a permanently ingrained preservation ethos. It has spawned 60 to 70 percent of all archaeological employment and is in the process of reconfiguring professional priorities within our own community. Yes, there have been quantum leaps in pure research, from our knowledge of human origins and hominid dispersals to the origins of agriculture and sedentism, urban organization, and site formation process. None of these compare to the significance of preservation in fashioning the direction of our profession. Just think about the intimate ambiance of meetings 20 years ago and the topics that were discussed. If we had continued to develop along the lines of a limited, academically oriented profession, our numbers would be reduced by two-thirds and our struggle for survival in the "de-academized" world of the global marketplace would be nothing short of ugly.

History also tells us that our profession's involvement as the NHPA unfolded was only marginally beneficial. Years of isolation in museums, universities, and research institutes left us ill prepared to structure the initial programs that begged for our expertise. Of course, there were exceptions and I believe that in the long run we have acquitted ourselves better in fashioning our fate than many would allow. A good number of us are now experts on areas ranging from preservation law to business ethics, administration, and entrepreneurship—but not enough. Decisions are still being largely made for us by bureaucrats and should be for as long as we decide that we should simply be pursuing business as usual. Changing that perception is what the SAA's Task Force on Curriculum is attempting to do.

The upside is that the struggles of the past 30 years have furnished an excellent baseline for rectifying the situation because most of us are really fairly intelligent and hopefully our perceptions have been honed by our failures and successes during what I would call the first stage of the CRM Revolution. However, lest we be doomed to repeat our previous failures, the watch words for archaeology well into the next century must be *Preservation* and *Cultural Resource Management.* Moreover, because of increasing globalization, preservation and CRM will extend into international spheres in which heritage tourism will play an even more pivotal role. The lion's share of our programs for restructuring archeological education must keep these concerns paramount.

I proceed to examine the ways in which my colleagues on the task force have proposed that traditional programs be modified.

Undergraduate Education

I wholeheartedly agree with the observations, and most significantly, with the priorities set by the task force. Indeed, fostering stewardship of resources and conveying the message that archaeologists are not the sole proprietors of those resources are the most critical lessons to be conveyed. Undergraduates are still learning the basic lessons of heritage, respect for interethnic differences, and ethics. Most will not become archaeologists, but surprisingly many, as our experience shows, will interface with preservation personnel over the course of their professional careers (i.e., planners, engineers, environmental regulators, and even accountants). They must have a groundwork that enables them to ask the right questions of archaeological professionals. The need to hone written oral and communication skills is self-evident. This is part and parcel of a well-rounded liberal arts education and must be emphasized in archaeology programs as it must in other curricula for the social sciences, humanities, and even the physical sciences.

The main issue in a major's undergraduate education should be the development of the intellect. My feeling is that courses in such sexy and exciting avenues as early hominids, early civilization, and pre-European cultures of the New World should form the core of any undergraduate major in archaeology. Junior- and senior-level work should include more comprehensive work in preservation and archaeological ethics; these can be courses cross-listed with introductory graduate offerings. It also would provide the advanced undergraduate with a taste of what "real-world" archaeology is all about.

On a broad scale, I would argue that the state of undergraduate education in the United States is on a considerably sounder footing than those of postgraduate education and professional development.

Graduate Education

We are on a disastrous collision course in graduate education, with little immediate hope for relief. The discipline is short of funding, universities are cutting budget lines, and programs that "demonstrably do not lead to jobs in anthropology" are in serious danger. More disturbingly, we are considered "irrelevant and self-indulgent." This situation is not about to change unless we make ourselves relevant and realign most programs to reflect practical skills in contemporary, high-tech archaeology as well as skills that will be required in the commercial world.

Yet our programs are structured under the assumption that realignment of programs does not matter. Many professors remain oblivious to overhauls because in the short term their stakes in change are perceived as self-defeating. Research in "glamor" areas is accomplished by senior faculty and nothing else matters. Elsewhere I have argued that on an intellectual plane there is a difference between constantly rethinking archaeology and "doing it," which is the path that must be pursued in CRM.

The bottom line is that we need to *do archaeology* and do it efficiently. Of course, we need to think about it, but we need to do our cognitive work as we move along in the practice of survey, testing, and excavation. More significantly, the new engine driving archaeology is not the research institute or funding agency but state and federal coffers whose charge is dictated by preservation law and compliance. For the profession generally, research agendas are no longer selected by professors; they are imposed by planners.

However, the dominant academic paradigm is, as per the popular refrain, "stuck in the '60s." Despite restructuring in the archaeological workplace and priorities, major departments still dedicate their efforts to training students to become researchers and teachers. The continued production of growing numbers of students to fill dwindling academic slots is misinformed at best and deceitful at worst. Yet it goes on.

The time-worn argument that a university's mission is to teach archaeologists to think and not to serve as vocational training grounds begs the issue sorely and bespeaks elitist arrogance, at a time when the cost, effort, and duration of Ph.D. programs is greater than it ever has been and offerings for traditional jobs have never been as meager. Informal surveys of graduate programs show that the course types taught at most institutions do not differ qualitatively from those taught over the past 30 years. Introductory core courses are followed by "method and theory" offerings reflecting the specialty and regional interests of the professors who teach at a given institution rather than the interests of the students.

University archaeological programs offer nothing or little in the way of practical courses that prepare students for the job market. Rest assured that the sophisticated CRM firms of today will not and should not invest in training prestigious recent Ph.D.s who cannot operate a Total Station or track a budget. Why hire a Ph.D. expert in Old World ceramics when many master's-level students knows how to run a shovel test crew and have intimate knowledge of landowner concerns? This is not to say that students do not pick up practical skills along the way; most do. However, they do this not because of the formal requirements of a department, but sometimes in spite of it. For survival reasons, students must pick up "job skills" that will require them to ease into the CRM world. Yet, they often do this at the expense of advancing in degree programs, at the risk of incurring the wrath of advisers and violating department protocol, and on their own time. The dilemma is especially grievous for long-term students (i.e., those in Ph.D. programs) where structure is eliminated after attainment of ABD status and the march to the dissertation is a long, energy-consuming, and often obsessive ordeal that leaves little time for the pursuit of employment-related training.

The real question before us is: where do we go from here? My concern is that many of us know the answer, but, for a variety of reasons, we may either be hesitant or even fearful to pose the solution. Drastic solutions have already been proposed that get to the core of the entire structure of graduate education (not only in anthropology but across the board in the humanities, social sciences, and perhaps, most strikingly, the hard sciences). Solutions have been proposed by figures no less influential than university presidents and deans of divisions and have been published in high-profile articles in the *New York Times*, *Atlantic Monthly*, and *Business Week*. In most cases, these individuals are less motivated by their own grand visions than by the rules of the market which are effectively saying across the board "less is more." Because of restructured job markets and the scaling down of the academy, proposals center on de-emphasis on the Ph.D. and refocusing on the M.A. which should become the "driver's license" or union card for all positions of senior responsibility in commercial entities engaging in professional practices.

Action Items.

1) *Reduce the number of Ph.D.s awarded.* There are too many out there and they are not needed.

2) *Reorient the master's degree.* This should be a complete and comprehensive degree and not just another whistle stop on the glorious road to the Ph.D.

3) *Revamp course requirements for archaeologists in anthropology departments to include offerings in other fields in such areas as preservation law, ethics, business, and proposal writing.* Mandatory revisions to archaeology curricula also would include courses on statistics, sampling, and GIS, all skills that will be indispensable in the next few years.

4) *Initiate formal internship programs between universities and CRM companies and/or governmental agencies.* These would be required for degree programs and officially recognized by departments in the form of credits and satisfaction of formal requirements.

5) *Develop courses and programs in public education that will enable students to interact with local communities.* Students should be encouraged to pursue careers that will bring them in touch with the public, the eventual source of most archeological funding in the long term.

6) *Replace open faculty lines (through retirement, attrition, or tenure elimination) by accomplished CRM professionals.* The latter would be capable of teaching CRM and more general courses. Critically, they should be able to offer career advancement guidance to graduate students.

Postgraduate Education/Professional Development

It is folly for even the most seasoned and accomplished professional to assume that he or she is beyond retooling, especially in this technologically accelerated world, where most of us are painfully aware that our kids will outstrip us in techno-competence by the time they are in high school. Irrespective of our archaeological and professional situations, updates in knowledge and skills is requisite for the competitive edge. This is applicable to teaching as well as to ground- and laboratory-based archaeology.

Action Item. Emphasis on encouraging dissertation and thesis topics on stewardship and preservation issues is critical if we are to develop technologies and strategies to cope with expanding databases. Preservation initiatives will go nowhere unless we learn to digest our data and interpret the masses of information that are entering our repositories every day. It simply will be embarrassing to plan program expansions if we prove to be incapable of handling the present influx of information.

Action Item. We must develop systematic methods for handling conflict resolution and for enhancing human interaction skills. We are notorious for our skills in handling dead things and tripping over live ones. Public relations will be an increasingly critical component of an archeological career; there is absolutely no reason that this element of our work should not be formally placed in a curriculum.

Action Item. Regulatory courses and seminars should be constantly upgraded because of the fluid regulatory environment. Familiarity with all the kinks in the process by practicing and teaching professionals also is mandatory. All practitioners need to be involved; none should be exempt.

Conclusions

The horizons of archaeology are expanding. The potential tragedy is that we will not have the supply of well-trained, contemporary practitioners to cope with the glut. I turn your attention especially to the expanding arena of international CRM in which heritage conservation and tourism will be the next major focus of attention. This is already happening in many parts of the world; the recent World Archaeological Congress (WAC) conference in South Africa underscored the great strides that are being made. Pay especial attention to developments in Third World countries where tourism and monuments will be the most immediate resources for financially strapped economies; classic examples are China, Egypt, India, Mexico, Pakistan, Peru, and Central and Eastern Europe. On the positive side, the emergence of an intricate but increasingly efficient preservation program in the United States can place us on the cutting edge of international CRM development, given (ironically, in light of my foregoing comments), our success in redirecting governmental priorities. My own experience is that we have done very well with a comparatively small and unglamorous archaeological resource base. Other countries have many more and longer-standing cultural resources, but they have less managerial, technological, and financial resources at their disposal. The opportunity is there.

However, before we can develop grandiose plans and projects, it is crucial that we get our own house in order. We need to streamline undergraduate education and instill the preservation ethic into courses and programs for both majors and non-majors. Nonspecialists will only benefit by learning exactly what it is that we do. Graduate programs remain the major source of concern. We do our brightest students no justice by drilling them with antiquated theories, methodologies, and information that is of limited utility. The ultimate insult is a career path that now averages 12 years (post-bachelor's), grows longer, and provides fewer opportunities at a time when the reverse is true for the profession as a whole. Nothing short of a restructuring of programs, faculty appointments, and long-term internship programs is viable at this time. Professional re-education is vital if the present leadership is to keep pace with the developments of tomorrow.

Ultimately, the decision-making processes rest with those members of the archaeological community that are setting the course of our profession. As archaeologists, we will not be true to our calling if we do not heed the past lessons of our own professional culture. If we really want to "save the past for the future," we will not repeat its mistakes. In basic terms, this means fashioning our own future before someone else does it for us.

Archaeologists as Anthropologists: The Question of Training

David G. Anderson

In spite of the massive changes our profession has undergone in the past 30 years, the way we train archaeology students has remained essentially the same as it was 30, 40, or even 50 years ago. That is, within anthropology departments, which continue to produce the vast majority of the archaeologists working in this country, students are trained first as anthropologists, and only secondarily as archaeologists.

The relevance of the traditional four-field (i.e., archaeology, cultural anthropology, linguistics, and physical anthropology) approach to the training of archaeologists has been questioned, particularly for archaeologists heading for nonacademic positions. It has been noted that much of what is taught in the four traditional subfields (*including archaeology*), has little or no utility to the practice of archaeology today. The core of this argument appears to revolve around the perception that teaching courses in linguistics, cultural anthropology, and physical anthropology takes up valuable time that would be better spent imparting more useful information and skills to our students.

Subsumed within this is the fundamental question, "Should archaeology remain within anthropology?"—that is, do archaeologists need to be trained as anthropologists? That much of the subject matter that is taught in many anthropology courses today is perceived as trivial, arcane, or otherwise irrelevant to many practicing archaeologists is unquestioned. That archaeology in this country is now increasingly practiced by people whose primary graduate training has been a field other than anthropology, such as American studies, classics, geography, history, or some other related discipline, also is undeniable, and further negates the position that training in anthropology is essential to doing archaeology.

The counter-argument, that anthropology is relevant in archaeological training, has been perhaps best expressed by Kent Flannery (1982), in his classic "Golden Marshalltown" article. In this paper, Flannery argued that the concept of culture (encompassing all four subfields) was an essential unifying framework for scholars responsible for finding, documenting, and interpreting the remains left behind by past cultural systems, and produced by a wide range of behaviors. Anthropology teaches a holistic view of human behavior, and some exposure to the discipline is probably essential to the training of an effective archaeologist. You can indeed find employment in archaeology without any training in anthropology, but you can do archaeology better if you have been educated within an anthropological framework.

Specific Training Options

Given this situation, and the exigencies of real-world academic politics, it is likely that a middle-ground approach might work best, involving the development and teaching of courses, as McGimsey (1994) has suggested, in subjects such as "Linguistics for Archaeologists," "Physical Anthropology for Archaeologists," "Cultural Anthropology for Archaeologists," and even "Anthropology for Archaeologists." Such an approach might help reduce the anomie felt sometimes by archaeology students when forced to learn the nuances of generative-transformational grammar, cognitive anthropology, or human genetics. I would suggest that archaeologists are themselves not free of sin in the teaching of their own subject matter. Many of us could benefit from a course or two on the application of archaeological theory to real-world field, analysis, and reporting situations.

In revamping the academic curricula for archaeologists, there are additional areas where change might be profitably made. For example, when scholars need to acquire a foreign language, they are likely to learn it without being required to do so. The elimination of the language requirement at the master's level might free up time for more archaeology courses. In addition, specific courses that could be offered to archaeologists could include preservation law and management, GIS/computer applications, statistical analyses/quantitative methods, business management skills, and technical writing. Likewise, archaeological ethics must receive a high priority, with an emphasis on our obligations to the archaeological record, to reporting our findings responsibly, and to our subjects and audience, including the descendants of the peoples under study.

Stewardship, public education and outreach, and the widespread dissemination of our findings are also areas that must receive greater emphasis in a revitalized archaeological program. As McGimsey and Davis note in this volume, "public archaeology IS archaeology," and we might as well start educating students in that fact. That is, what we do must be better understood. A majority of the people employed in archaeology in the United States today are involved in resource management/stewardship, at a great cost of public and private funds. This fact, however, is not well reflected in the contents of our journals or even in opinion polls, news coverage, or PBS specials about what it is that archaeologists do. What we do is much more than a high-tech way to find neat things, yet that is the perception of our field among much of the general public.

Accordingly, perhaps the single most important thing we must teach, particularly in our introductory courses, is the value of archaeology itself. At the introductory (i.e., undergraduate) level, our subject matter must be presented in such a way that we attract and create advocates, not bore them into antipathy. Our subject matter is inherently interesting to a great many people, and we should take advantage of this fact.

How do we inform the general public about what it is archaeologists do and why it is important? We can make a good start by using our introductory courses as proselytizing as well as educational forums. The authors of good fiction about our field such as Piers Anthony, Jean M. Auel, and Michael and Kathleen Gear have introduced more people to life in the past than most professional archaeologists ever will. Their works could be introduced and (critically but favorably) discussed in our courses. We thus need to support the accurate popularization of our profession, as the SAA's Public Education Committee and the various state archaeology day/week/month coordinators are doing so well.

At the advanced undergraduate and graduate level, the education of archaeologists needs to be made relevant to real-world concerns. We need courses that can teach us how to excavate sites to maximize information recovery and write up the results; to develop realistic and achievable research designs and historic preservation plans; to deal with the ethical dilemmas raised by life in the moneyed world of big-business cultural resource management (CRM); and to understand why it is critical to take and curate good notes, photographs, and analysis records along with artifact collections.

Good CRM reports need to be held up as examples to students, who in turn need to be taught how to produce such documents. More of us need to know where the money that is spent on archaeology really comes from, so we can shape what is available and how it gets spent. More students need to be interns in CRM firms, state historic preservation offices, or government agencies, and many educators could benefit by the same exposure. We need people who can understand how systematic shovel testing can yield information important to understanding past cultural systems. We need to develop people who can quickly take threatened sites apart and learn important things from them, not just trowel out the levels in 1-meter squares or neatly wash and label artifacts.

In the years ahead, we will need to deal with threatened sites on an unprecedented scale. We need people who aren't afraid to make hard choices in the field—the literal triage of sites and features—to maximize information recovery. Far too often the hand excavation of block units is considered effective mitigation on sites of all sizes and with all kinds of deposits. Use of heavy equipment to expose large numbers of features, however, is more preferable than having a few scattered telephone booths, with no real clue about the kind of site these units passed through.

We need to develop a greater preservation ethic about where and how we do our work. Too many field schools and research projects are conducted on protected sites, recovering trivial bits of data while major sites are going under all around. More efforts should be devoted to threatened sites, to quickly and efficiently recover large quantities of data of relevance to major research questions.

Besides educating and training in doing CRM itself, we need to be producing people capable of the monitoring and peer review necessary to ensure that high-quality work occurs. Many agency and SHPO reviewers need training in how to review——that is, learning how to focus on what is important, such as do the conclusions and recommendations follow from the data, what can we learn from these sites, and what is the best way to collect this kind of information? Management recommendations coming from CRM work should be directed to either preserving sites or maximizing information recovery. It is usually far cheaper to stabilize sites than to excavate them, but this option is rarely taught. Fieldwork must be based on information return, not employment potential. The importance of sound curation, specifically artifact and records management, also must be emphasized in our courses.

Instituting Change

To institute change will requires action on the part of a great many individuals; collective action is, after all, the sum of individual actions. In revitalizing the teaching of archaeology, having the SAA and other leading bodies of our profession endorse a call for change is an essential step, but that will not be enough. Change will have to come class by class and department by department, and will require individuals to make stands about what will be taught, who will be hired, and how promotion will occur. We must all be agents for change; the situation is not one in which we can afford to sit back and let others carry the burden.

The hiring and promotion of good people is critically important. Departments need to hire people who will teach practical, real-world skills in their courses, who understand what modern archaeology entails and can impart this knowledge to their students. We need to reward with tenure those who do this well. Likewise, we need to reward faculty members who undertake public service and education efforts, or who produce major contributions to knowledge rather than large numbers of articles. A good site report is used forever, while a good theoretical article has a half life of about five years at best. At present, however, someone who writes the latter will get tenure, while the author of the former will likely get the street.

The impact of hiring and promotion policies, of course, operates in a Darwinian fashion and over a period of many years. Well-trained students will be hired, the poorly trained ignored. As awareness of these basic facts of life spread, enrollments in departments will rise or fall. Change may come if we work towards it, but it will not always occur quickly or easily. Changing our educational system is thus in many ways akin to the way paradigm shifts occur in science...through the conversion or replacement of personnel.

Effecting change also requires political astuteness, the ability to sell a point of view to people. In this regard, some training in politics is essential, not only to effect change at the national level, but also within our own professional and academic communities. If we wish to sell our case for change to our anthropological colleagues, one way to do this is by emphasizing what's in it for them, namely continued enrollment and possibly even departmental survival. Co-opting rather than confronting our colleagues, and showing respect for and value in what they do, is likely to be a more effective strategy than challenging their subfield's very relevance. That is why a middle-ground approach will work best, taking what is relevant from our anthropological heritage, rather than divorcing ourselves from it completely.

Making Archaeology Relevant

Anthropology, and archaeology within it, needs to rise to the challenges facing the modern world if it is to remain credible, just as earlier generations of anthropologists like Boas, Benedict, and Kroeber pursued the big questions, and argued passionately against racism and injustice and for cultural relativism. Archaeology can take a leading role in such activities. Major issues that need addressing include climate change and its impact on human society, genocide and racism, the recognition and protection of cultural diversity, and sound resource management (stewardship). We need to explore these issues wherever possible in our research and writings, and teach them to our students.

Archaeology can contribute greatly to understanding the effects of environmental degradation and climate change on human society. Using dendrochronological data, for example, it is possible to compare recent weather patterns with those for the past thousand or more years in the southeastern and southwestern United States, and how annual rainfall variation affected both crop production and political stability in a wide range of local societies. Examining the impacts of the mid-Holocene warm interval may help us better understand what we might have to look forward to given global warming, and finer scale analyses may help resolve the effects of El Niño and other periodic climatic fluctuations on human societies.

As a profession we also need to confront and reject our sometimes paternalistic/colonialistic attitudes. Archaeology is not intended to be confrontational, the teaching of benighted or ignorant peoples a "true" history of the past, capable of replacing (implied) illusory traditions. People have every reason to react strongly when their core beliefs are challenged, and archaeologists have to moderate their arguments about what it is they do. Alternative ways of perceiving time and the past are important ways of being human that should be championed, not denigrated. How time, space, and place are perceived, parenthetically, no doubt also profoundly shaped the archaeological record, and offers another way to approach an understanding of it.

We thus need to have better relations with the people whose past we study, be they black, white, red, or yellow. We must come to respect and educate each other about our goals and values, however, rather than lamenting or casting recriminations back and forth. Recognizing that some repatriation and reburial of remains is going to occur, we need to redouble our analyses of existing collections. Many of the classic assemblages in southeastern archeology, particularly materials gathered during the Mound Exploration work of the Smithsonian Institution's Bureau of Ethnology, for example, have never been adequately described or illustrated. Our students need to be taught that digging isn't all that we need do to legitimize ourselves as archaeologists; there are many honorable specializations to choose from, including curation, records management, and the analysis of earlier collections.

As archaeologists we study the causes of long-term change in cultural systems, of which organizational change has been something of a hot topic in recent years. Now is the time to apply some of the lessons we have learned. We must continue to emphasize solutions and problem solving wherever possible, lighting candles rather than cursing the darkness. The future is ours to shape.

References Cited

Flannery, K. V.
1982   The Golden Marshalltown: A Parable for the Archaeology of the 1980s. *American Anthropologist* 84:265-278.

McGimsey, C. R. III
1994   The Yin and Yang of Archaeology. *Newsletter of the Society for Professional Archaeologists* 18(10):1-4

McGimsey, C. R. III, and H. A. Davis
2000   The Old Order Changeth; Or, Now that Archaeology is in the Deep End of the Pool, Let's Not Just Tread Water. In *Teaching Archaeology in the Twenty-First Century,* edited by Susan J. Bender and George S. Smith, pp 5-8. Society for American Archaeology, Washington, D.C.

VI.
WHERE DO WE GO FROM HERE?

A CALL TO ACTION

The main emphasis of the SAA's Task Force on Curriculum to this point has been to begin to frame the important issue of educating and training archaeologists for the challenges of the twenty-first century. Discussions included the role of undergraduate and graduate programs in this effort, as well as the requirement that practicing archaeologists keep up with changing methods, theory, and technology. Workshops have been held, sessions at professional meetings have been organized, and information has been exchanged through articles in professional publications and the Internet. All these efforts have been designed to identify and articulate the issues and to frame them within the context of a diverse archaeological community. That process continues with this report.

This report is not intended to be the final word but rather a continuation and hopefully an escalation of the National Dialogue already under way. To ensure that the diversity of opinion is brought to bear on this issue the SAA has established a Bulletin Board on Teaching Archaeology in the twenty-first century on its Web site. Make your concerns known. Log onto this site and provide your comments and suggestions. You can log on through the SAA's Home Page or directly at http://www.saa.org/Education/Curriculum. Comments will be used to prepare various reports, articles, and proposals on this topic and to direct the curriculum reform process.

The task force hopes that this report will stimulate discussions with colleagues and students about the future direction of archaeology and that departments will be encouraged to review programs, courses, and faculty lines within the context of what has been discussed here. This is truly an issue that permeates the entire profession regardless of how it is practiced. Change will only be brought about by the collective efforts of the entire archaeological community. If archaeology is to meet the challenges of the twenty-first century, now is the time to Stop, Look, and Listen. We need the vision and leadership of the professional community and the dedication, wonder, and passion of those preparing for careers in archaeology to ensure that archaeology is viable and relevant in the new millennium and beyond.

ABOUT THE CONTRIBUTORS

Jeffrey H. Altschul is president of Statistical Research, Inc., in Tucson, Arizona.

David G. Anderson is an archaeologist with the Southeast Archeological Center, National Park Service, in Tallahassee, Florida.

Susan J. Bender is associate dean of the faculty and professor at anthropology at Skidmore College in Saratoga Springs, New York.

Judith A. Bense is director of the Archaeological Institute at the University of West Florida in Pensacola.

Dennis B. Blanton is director of the Center for Archaeological Research at the College of William & Mary in Williamsburg.

Kathleen M. Byrd is head, Department of Social Sciences and professor of anthropology at Northwestern State University of Louisiana in Natchitoches.

Pam Cressey is city archaeologist in Alexandria, Virginia.

Hester A. Davis is state archaeologist emeritus at the Arkansas Archeological Survey in Fayetteville.

Ricardo J. Elia is director of the Office of Public Archaeology at Boston University.

Brian M. Fagan is a professor in the Department of Anthropology at the University of California, Santa Barbara.

Dorothy Schlotthauer Krass is the former manager, public education, at the Society for American Archaeology in Washington, D.C.

William D. Lipe is a professor in the Department of Anthropology at Washington State University in Pullman.

Mark J. Lynott is manager of the Midwest Archeological Center, National Park Service, in Lincoln, Nebraska.

Charles R. McGimsey III is director emeritus of the Arkansas Archeological Survey in Fayetteville.

Francis P. McManamon is chief archaeologist and departmental consulting archaeologist with the National Park Service in Washington, D.C.

James J. Miller is state archaeologist for Florida, based in the Department of State in Tallahassee.

K. Anne Pyburn is an associate professor in the Department of Anthropology at Indiana University in Bloomington.

Joseph Schuldenrein is president of Geoarchaeology Research Associates in New York.

George S. Smith is an archaeologist with the Southeast Archeological Center, National Park Service, in Tallahassee, Florida.

Dean R. Snow is professor and head of the Department of Anthropology at Penn State University.

Vincas P. Steponaitis is a professor in the Department of Anthropology at the University of North Carolina, Chapel Hill.

Joe Watkins is agency archaeologist of the Bureau of Indian Affairs-Anadarko Agency in Oklahoma.

Nancy Marie White is an associate professor in the Department of Anthropology at the University of South Florida in Tampa.